The Wakamatsu Tea and Silk Colony Farm and the Creation of Japanese America

The Wakamatsu Tea and Silk Colony Farm and the Creation of Japanese America

Daniel A. Métraux

Foreword by Amy S. Miller
Afterword by Melissa Lobach

LEXINGTON BOOKS
Lanham • Boulder • New York • London

Published by Lexington Books
An imprint of The Rowman & Littlefield Publishing Group, Inc.
4501 Forbes Boulevard, Suite 200, Lanham, Maryland 20706
www.rowman.com

6 Tinworth Street, London SE11 5AL

Copyright © 2019 by The Rowman & Littlefield Publishing Group, Inc.

All rights reserved. No part of this book may be reproduced in any form or by any electronic or mechanical means, including information storage and retrieval systems, without written permission from the publisher, except by a reviewer who may quote passages in a review.

British Library Cataloguing in Publication Information Available

Library of Congress Cataloging-in-Publication Data

ISBN: 978-1-4985-8538-5 (cloth)
ISBN: 978-1-4985-8539-2 (electronic)
ISBN: 978-1-4985-8540-8 (pbk.)

I dedicate this book to the American River Conservancy in recognition of their fine work in restoring and recovering the history of the Wakamatsu Colony and for their work in making the Wakamatsu Farm an enduring success today.

I am deeply grateful for the advice, assistance, and strong encouragement I received from the staff and volunteer docents at the American River Conservancy in Coloma. Special thanks to Melissa Lobach and Wendy Guglieri for their help, advice, corrections, and deep patience and Melissa's fine Afterword.

Contents

Foreword *Amy S. Miller*		ix
Acknowledgments		xi
Introduction		1
1	National Tension That Brought on the Boshin War in Japan and Refugees from the Aizu Domain to California	17
2	John Henry Schnell's Service to the Aizu Domain and His Decision to Move to California	31
3	Japanese Immigration to the United States	39
4	The Founding of the Wakamatsu Tea and Silk Colony Farm	51
5	The Wakamatsu Dream: A Diverse and Flourishing Agricultural Community	65
6	The Last Days of the Wakamatsu Tea and Silk Colony Farm	77
7	The Creation of the Legendary Okei-San	91
8	Wakamatsu as a Pilgrimage Site	101
9	What Happened to the Wakamatsu Colonists?	107
Afterword: Conserving Wakamatsu Farm—American River Conservancy *Melissa Lobach*		113
Appendix I: Application to Place the Wakamatsu Colony Farm on the National Register of Historic Places in 2009		121

Appendix II: Text of the Deed of the Sale of Land by Charles M.
    Graner to J. Henry Schnell: June 18, 1869   133

Bibliography   135

Index   139

About the Author   145

Foreword

Amy S. Miller

In recent years the subject of American immigration has sparked a great deal of heated public discourse. Who should have the right to enter the United States and how? What kind of policies should the country maintain at its borders? What rights should noncitizens have access to and what pathways should exist for those eligible for citizenship? Indeed, who constitutes the "we" of "We the people"? Who gets to decide? Such debates over who Americans are and who can become "us" are not recent inventions. Even a brief look at U.S. immigration history, for instance, reveals the continual tension between the welcoming of newcomers and the diversity they bring versus expressions of concern and fear over the ways new immigrants might change or threaten "American" life.

Against the backdrop of these dual impulses, each community has its stories to tell of struggles and triumphs in the process of arriving on America's shores and the journey to becoming a part of American society. For Japanese Americans, the narrative of their success also contains what is, no doubt, one of the saddest chapters in American history and one of the grossest violations of civil rights in the twentieth century—President Franklin D. Roosevelt's forced relocation of Japanese Americans into internment camps during World War II. The momentous decision to send certain citizens to concentration camps solely on the basis of race had a long-lasting impact on Japanese American communities and still resonates for many Japanese Americans to this day. Unfortunately, the history and impact of this tragic era is often glossed over or minimalized as a side note in studies of American history. Preserving the memory of internment, therefore, has become important for Japanese American activists seeking to expose the truth, educate the public, and prevent such injustices from happening again.

While the story and poignant lesson of the internment camps must never be forgotten, it is not the place where the Japanese American story begins. By the time of World War II, Japanese immigrants had long established themselves in the United States and had transformed the communities in which they had settled. In the present monograph, Dr. Daniel A. Metraux, Professor of Asian Studies at Mary Baldwin University, turns to the first moments of this narrative by offering a rich and detailed history of the Wakamatsu Tea and Silk Colony Farm, often remembered as the birthplace of Japanese Americans. Although the colony ultimately failed, the attempts by Japanese immigrants to create such a place speak to their courage and pioneering spirit, signaling the many Japanese who followed in their wake. Metraux's exceptional study of this colony not only serves as a step forward in understanding how and why the Japanese first came to the United States, it speaks to the important legacy that Japanese peoples would impart in becoming a part of American life.

Amy S. Miller
Assistant Professor of Asian Studies
Mary Baldwin University
Staunton, Virginia
Summer 2018

Acknowledgments

Many colleagues and friends played an important role in the development of this work. My daughter, Katie Metraux, a long time official at California State Parks, introduced me to many of the sites where Asians established viable communities in the nineteenth century and told me about the site of the Wakamatsu Colony near Coloma. Katie has played a vital role in State Park's work to preserve such historic sites as Jack London's home, Fort Ross, Angel Island, and so much more.

When I presented a short conference paper on the Wakamatsu experience in January 2017, Asian historian John Van Sant told me about his extensive research and writing on the subject. A chapter in his 2000 book *Pacific Pioneers* on the Wakamatsu Colony was the strong launching pad that led to this research. I am very grateful for Dr. Van Sant's later strong encouragement and suggestions for improvements.

I deeply appreciate the help received from the editors of Lexington Books including former editor Brian Hill who spotted my paper on Wakamatsu in an Asian Studies conference program and who suggested that I should do a book on the topic. Thanks also to Acquisitions Editor Eric Kuntzman.

Many colleagues read extensive portions of this manuscript at various stages of writing and provided many invaluable comments and suggestions. They include Professors Rick Plant and Amy Miller at Mary Baldwin University, Harris Dillon, William Head, Paul Capobianco, and Douglas Clark. Special thanks to Dr. Miller for her excellent foreword.

I am deeply grateful for the advice, assistance, and strong encouragement I received from the staff and volunteer docents at the American River Conservancy in Coloma. Special thanks to Melissa Lobach and Wendy Guglieri for their help, advice, corrections, and deep patience.

Introduction

A large stone memorial on the grounds of the Gold Trail Elementary School at Gold Hill in northern California, dedicated in June 1969 by then Governor Ronald Reagan, succinctly tells the tale of the first planned Japanese settlement in North America:

> Wakamatsu Tea and Silk Farm Colony
>
> Site of the only tea and silk farm in California. First agricultural settlement of pioneer Japanese immigrants who arrived at Gold Hill on June 8, 1869. Despite the initial success, it failed. It marked the beginning of Japanese influence on the agricultural economy of California.

This work is a study of the circumstances that led to the founding of the colony, its initial success and ultimate failure, and how the site has become a major pilgrimage center for ethnic Japanese.

Anthropologist Margaret Mead once observed that every cultural group has its own creation story. People need to know where they came from, how they evolved from the past. These roots can create a sense of bonding and belonging that marks them as part of a greater family that is distinct from other cultures. These creation stories may be based on actual happenings, encapsulated in some form of mythology or some combination of myth and fact. Whenever Mead studied a new culture, one of the first things she attempted was to ascertain how they viewed their own origins. Discovering that would tell the anthropologist a lot about that culture's specific world-view.[1]

The story of the Wakamatsu Colony is a good case study of how a failed experiment to create a sustainable Japanese colony in California became a virtual shrine for the creation of a large Japanese American community in the United States.

Japanese Americans have their own unique cultural values as well as their own creation myths. There was a massive migration of well over one hundred thousand Japanese from their homeland to North America from the mid-1800s to the mid-1920s with many settling in California. When the original *Issei* (first-generation) reached old age in the 1920s, many sought to leave a written record of their accomplishments in the New World. Their published histories tended to emphasize well-educated and well-bred immigrants whose hard work and virtuous values created a heroic group of settlers who moved from success to success as pioneers who tamed the wilderness and contributed mightily to California's booming agricultural economy. They largely ignored the fact that many of the early male immigrants were impoverished farmers who had little or no formal education and that many of the female immigrants were prostitutes who plied their trade near work stations housing Japanese and Chinese workers.

When these Japanese-American historians in the 1920s carefully studied the history of Japanese settlement in North America, they occasionally heard about a group of approximately thirty Japanese farmers and carpenters led by a German entrepreneur named John Henry Schnell (c. 1841–?) who attempted to create a permanent Japanese colony in northern California in 1869. The goal of the Wakamatsu Tea and Silk Colony Farm, located in the community of Gold Hill near Placerville and Coloma, California, was to produce Japanese-style tea and silk for the American market. The venture eventually failed, but it served as a harbinger for a much greater wave of Japanese that was to come a generation later.

One of the Wakamatsu Farm settlers was a teenage girl, Okei Ito (c. 1852–1871; also referred to as Okei-san), who came to California with a group of Japanese workers to care for the two infant daughters of Schnell and his Japanese wife. Okei-san died shortly after the 1871 collapse of the Wakamatsu Farm and was buried on a small hill overlooking the farm property. A number of Japanese American writers as well as a novelist and movie producer in Japan in the 1930s transformed Okei-san into a virtuous and saintly heroine, a modern-day Joan of Arc, who led the first wave of Japanese pioneers to California. She died a heroic death at a tender age but served as the inspiration that brought other Japanese to America.

Today many ethnic Japanese make the long pilgrimage to Gold Hill, the site of the Wakamatsu Farm and Okei's grave, to honor their ancestors who later settled in North America. Many ethnic Japanese revere the Wakamatsu Colony for the same reasons that many Americans visit Plymouth Rock, so much so that the site has become an important pilgrimage center relating to the creation of Japanese America.

JAPANESE IMMIGRATION TO THE UNITED STATES

Japanese-American history is a vivid narrative of the immigration of many tens of thousands of Japanese to the American West during the last two decades of the nineteenth century and the early years of the twentieth century. The main thrust of this peaceful invasion began in the mid-1880s, but an earlier effort to establish an agricultural colony of native Japanese in northern California actually began in 1869. The Wakamatsu Tea and Silk Colony Farm disbanded in two years, but remains a fascinating and until now largely untold story that was a harbinger to the later deluge of immigration from Japan. This work details the reasons for the successes and failures of the Colony and the later myths which have transformed the settlement into a pilgrimage site for ethnic Japanese and the virtual canonization of a young Colony woman who became a figurative beacon for Japan's 1930s invasion of Manchuria and mainland China.

When several small groups of Japanese immigrated to California in 1869 and 1870, there had never been in the modern era any other known instances of Japanese leaving their home islands for a new life abroad. Emigration was not in the Japanese blood. Although Japanese officials began directing foreign policy initiatives soon after the Meiji Restoration in 1868, no one thought in terms of individuals actually leaving the archipelago. Foreign travel had been forbidden during the 250 years of Tokugawa control, and after two very unsuccessful attempts to export Japanese farm workers to Guam and Hawaii in 1868, the Japanese government absolutely forbade such forays abroad. Japanese were not likely to go out on their own. As one Hawaiian official noted sadly in 1881, "The Japanese are not an emigrating people."[2] This is why the attempt to create a Japanese colony in California in 1869 is so very unique.

The reasons for the founding of the Wakamatsu colony and the later massive emigration from Japan are very different. The Colony's participants fled the Aizu domain in Japan after imperial forces of the new Meiji government destroyed their homeland in the 1868–1869 Boshin civil war, which pitted the new government against bedrock supporters of the crumbling Tokugawa Shogunate. Led by German entrepreneur John Henry Schnell, up to thirty Japanese were desperate enough to defy Japanese law, which at that time forbade any Japanese to leave the country, in order to settle in an alien land far away. The later migrants were generally *dekasegi*, temporary workers who only intended to work long enough abroad to earn a good nest egg before returning home. However, many of them ultimately stayed in North America and Hawaii, often later sending for their families or "picture-brides."

This work investigates three phases of the history of the Wakamatsu Tea and Silk Colony Farm at Gold Hill, California. Established in June 1869, the

Colony served as the first Japanese settlement in North America. It enjoyed a promising start, but closed by June 1871, plagued by financial difficulties, contaminated water, and drought conditions. The second phase occurred in the 1920s and 1930s with the rediscovery of the colony by Japanese American historians. At this time Okei-san's grave and the farm property became a pilgrimage site for generations of ethnic Japanese who came there to honor their ancestors who had immigrated to the American West in the late nineteenth and early twentieth centuries. The third phase is now occurring in the early years of this century when the American River Conservancy (ARC) bought the property and began a long-term project to preserve the history of the colony and to restore the farm and to encourage modern agricultural use of the land.

Key themes include the reasons why approximately thirty Japanese immigrated to an alien California to create a farm colony and why they failed. A second area of exploration is how and why a solitary and long-forgotten young Japanese woman became a mythological symbol, a virtual patron saint representing the essence of Japanese nationhood and a beacon for Japan's invasion of Manchuria and for both Japanese-American historians as well as nationalist novelists and movie producers in Japan in the 1930s. A related chapter will explore how and when Okei-san's grave and the farm site became a key pilgrimage site for ethnic Japanese, as it remains to this day. This work concludes with a brief analysis of ARC's extensive efforts to restore the main house and to encourage the agricultural development of the land.

There are many issues to explore with each of these three phases of history. The first raises the question of why over two dozen Japanese would agree to travel to an alien land previously visited by only a handful of Japanese. What does it take to make such a community a success, and why did it ultimately fail? How did Americans react to the sudden presence of a colony of Japanese in their midst, and how does this reaction compare to the way Americans responded to the later migration of tens of thousands of Japanese to the American West?

Issues concerning the second phase start with the attempts of older first-generation Japanese (*Issei*) to write their history for later generations of Japanese Americans. Why did they feel the need to manufacture their own creation myths concerning the Wakamatsu colony and to transform a young common Japanese teenager and nurse into a saintly Joan of Arc figure leading the way for Japanese "pioneers" settling first in the wilds of California and later in Manchuria? How did the Wakamatsu colony site and Okei-san's grave become an important pilgrimage site for many Japanese and Japanese-Americans?

The third phase discussion focuses briefly on what the American River Conservancy hopes to do to reclaim both the land and the legacy of the Wakamatsu Colony. The question here is what it takes to honor the past by restoring the main farm house and other elements of the colony, while also reviving the land.

HISTORICAL OVERVIEW

The California Gold Rush that began in 1848 encouraged a wave of immigrants from China that numbered twenty-five thousand by 1852 and a great many more by 1880. By contrast, Japan's closed-door policy during the Edo or Tokugawa period (1600–1868) had forbidden the entry of most foreigners until the mid-1850s and the voluntary departure of any Japanese until 1885. The result was that with the exception of officially authorized groups sanctioned by the Japanese government and a few individuals, generally stranded Japanese sailors picked up by American ships, and students with government permission to study in the United States, there were virtually no Japanese anywhere in North America.

This taboo came to an end in May 1869, when a small group of Japanese arrived in San Francisco accompanied by a German-born arms dealer, John Henry (Heinrich) Schnell, his Japanese wife, Jou Schnell (c. 1845–?), and a young daughter, Frances. Their colony was the first planned group settlement of Japanese in North America who intended to settle there permanently Their objective was to create a large-scale farm that would produce Japanese-style tea and silk for sale in the American market. Their assumption was that since tea and silk were popular export items from Japan, there would be a ready market for those products produced in the United States. They became known as the Wakamatsu Tea and Silk Colony Farm.

The Japanese workers were most likely refugees from the Aizu Domain northeast of Tokyo. Aizu had sided with the Tokugawa Shogunate, which had ruled Japan since the early 1600s through to the start of the Boshin Civil War in 1868. This conflict was fought between Tokugawa forces and those seeking to return political power to the imperial court. Imperial forces laid waste to Aizu after an overwhelming military victory thereby forcing many of the Domain's surviving residents to seek new lives elsewhere. By the fall of 1870, there were an estimated twenty-five to thirty Japanese at the farm including women and children.

John Henry Schnell and his brother Edward most likely came to Japan in the early 1860s, where they engaged in various business operations, which by the mid- to late 1860s included the sale of weapons to several northern pro-Tokugawa domains. John Henry became an important conduit of arms for Aizu, where he settled by early 1868 and married the daughter of a local samurai. Following Aizu's defeat, John Henry lost his livelihood, which led him to concoct a scheme of creating a silk and tea farm in northern California.

When Schnell, his family, and several Japanese workers arrived at San Francisco, Schnell purchased a farm at Gold Hill, a small community near Placerville in the foothills of the Sierras. He quickly moved his group there, and commenced farmwork. The party, including Schnell's Japanese wife Jou,[3] arrived in San Francisco on May 27, 1869, aboard the side-wheeler PMSS *China* of the Pacific Mail Company. They were, in all likelihood, the first sizable group to arrive from Japan to settle in the continental United States. They soon traveled to Sacramento by riverboat and took wagons to Placerville and nearby Gold Hill. They brought with them thousands of tea plants, mulberry trees, silkworms, and other traditional crops to start a tea and silk operation.[4] They were later joined by two other groups of Japanese workers. After a successful start, the goal was to attract many more colonists from Wakamatsu who would expand the colony to a largely self-sustaining settlement that would produce silk, tea, rice, fish, wine, and other goods while serving as a refuge for displaced folk from Wakamatsu, the administrative center of Aizu domain.

The farm project initially showed some potential for success, but by early 1871 it became clear that it could no longer sustain its operations. Unfortunately, Schnell apparently came with insufficient funds to pay for the farm mortgage as well as farm materials and wages for the workers. Contaminated water and a prolonged drought killed many of the young plants. It is evident that by spring 1871 at least some of the Japanese workers began to drift away in search of other, better paying opportunities. The future whereabouts of many of the workers are largely unknown, but it is certain that at least some of them eventually returned to Japan.

Schnell, his wife, and two infant daughters left Gold Hill in June 1871 saying that they were going back to Japan to procure extra supplies and funding and that they would return to the farm, but they never came back and their ultimate fate is unknown. They left behind Okei Ito, a young Aizu woman whom they had hired as a nurse for their baby daughters as well as another male worker. Okei Ito moved in with a local farm family, but died from a fever later that summer of 1871. She was buried on a small hill overlooking the farm. It is believed that she may well have been the first Japanese woman and immigrant to die in North America.

The Wakamatsu colony was largely forgotten for over five decades until the early 1920s when several *Issei* historians writing about the massive immigration of Japanese into California starting in the mid-1880s made their way to Gold Hill. They celebrated the Wakamatsu colony as the birthplace of Japanese America and transformed Okei Ito (more commonly known as Okei-san) into a virtual shining puritanical saint and martyr who courageously led Japanese pioneers into the California wilderness. Over time, they made the colony site and Okei-san's grave into the major pilgrimage site for Japanese Americans.

The American River Conservancy bought the land in 2010 with several goals in mind. ARC is restoring the farmhouse and is making the grounds into a highly visible historic site. Its goal is to increase public awareness of this important place in American history. It is also encouraging the agricultural growth of the land and sponsors various events including pilgrimage visits by interested persons and groups.

WHY THE WAKAMATSU COLONY IS IMPORTANT IN THE HISTORY OF JAPANESE AMERICANS

Sacramento-based congressional representative Doris Matsui has stated that "to many Japanese Americans, the Wakamatsu Colony is as symbolic as Plymouth Rock was for the first American colonists."[5] Despite its short tenure, the Wakamatsu Colony has considerable historical significance. First, it was the initial attempt to create a large self-sustaining Japanese enclave in the United States before the first major waves of immigration in the 1880s. Second, they were the first group of Japanese who intended to settle permanently in North America. They initiated a trend which saw many later immigrants from Japan leaving their country, planning to stay away for good. Finally, although they did not directly influence the emigration from Japan a generation later, they were in fact the vanguard of *Issei* Japanese to North America.[6] Professor John E. Van Sant is correct when he notes, "While the colonists from Aizu had minimal direct influence on the course of relations between the United States and Japan, their departure from Japan as refugees, their intention to settle permanently in the United States, and their establishment of an agricultural colony would soon be imitated by thousands of Japanese immigrants."[7]

The Wakamatsu Colony gave many Americans their first chance to become acquainted with Japanese. By the late 1860s, over ten thousand Chinese had settled in the United States, but the Wakamatsu Japanese were comparative newcomers. Journalists began covering the Wakamatsu colonists quite literally the day of their first arrival in San Francisco. A stream of reporters visited them on a continual basis for the duration of their stay at Gold Hill. As was the custom at that time, other newspapers across the United States copied articles about the Japanese colonists, thus giving many other readers some information about these newest settlers.[8]

The American reaction to the arrival of the Wakamatsu Japanese was overwhelmingly positive. Journalists admired their pluck, hard work, education, skills, and enthusiasm. They applauded the Japanese colonists for "adopt[ing] the habits and customs of the American people."[9] Newspapers commented that the Japanese were trying to make an important contribution to the state's economic development while at the same time not threatening the jobs of American workers. In a nutshell, the fact that the number of Japanese was so small meant that they did not pose any economic, political, or social threat to the white Protestant hierarchy of this period.

These laudatory attitudes are very different from those of white Californians in the early decades of the twentieth century. We have here a very interesting case study of what happens when a new group of immigrants first comes to the United States. If their numbers are few and they behave in an appropriate manner, they are often welcomed with open arms, but if and when they come in large numbers, the reaction can become very negative. We see this over and over again with each new wave of immigrants into the United States.

The Wakamatsu colony also played a key role in the thinking, writing, and historical memory of later generations of ethnic Japanese in the United States. The center of attention was Okei-san, who probably came with the third group of Japanese in the summer or fall of 1870, but the fact that it represents a center for Japanese American pilgrimages is something that we must consider as well.

NATIONAL REGISTRY OF HISTORIC PLACES

The Wakamatsu Tea and Silk Colony Farm is listed on the National Register of Historic Places as a place of national historic significance. The 2009 application for this special recognition states: "The Wakamatsu Tea and Silk Colony Farm site is eligible for listing in the National Register under Criterion A at a national level of significance in the areas of ethnic heritage, agriculture, and early settlement."

The key to this recognition of the Wakamatsu Farm is that it was a harbinger of the huge Japanese immigration that would arrive in California between 1885 and 1907. The Japanese who came during this period prospered because of their experiences as farmers in Japan and their willingness to work hard in a highly productive manner. They introduced new methods of farming that had a major impact on California agriculture. According to the application for placement on the National Register:

> The contributions of the colony to California's agricultural industry are tied culturally to their Japanese heritage and include a focus on sericulture and tea, Japan's two most important export industries at the time the colony was established. While some prior experimentation with tea and silk farming had been attempted (by non-Japanese) in California, these efforts met with little success. Under the theme of Agriculture, the contributions of the Colony to the agriculture industry are recognized; they mark the beginning of Japanese influence on the agricultural economy of California and the United States. The Japanese colonists, like the later Japanese immigrants of the 1880s and 1890s, made

significant contributions to the agricultural development and crop specialization, particularly in the western United States.[10]

CHALLENGING THE SAMURAI MYTH

When I first learned about the Wakamatsu Tea and Silk Farm Colony, I turned to two online publications that purported to give an accurate historical account of the enterprise. The first site prepared by Sierranevadageo-tourism.org stated the following:

> In 1869, 22 samurai and their families emigrated from Japan to San Francisco. They traveled east and arrived at Gold Hill on 8 June 1869 to establish an agricultural settlement. They purchased land from Charles Graner with the help of John Henry Schnell to begin the first and only tea and silk farm in California at that time. The Wakamatsu Farm was the first Japanese Colony in North America.

I next went to Wikipedia and to my dismay found a fairly similar story:

> The Wakamatsu Tea and Silk Farm Colony was made up of a group of 22 samurai and one woman during the Boshin Civil War (1868–1869) in Japan preceding the Meiji Restoration. They are believed to be the first permanent Japanese settlement in North America and the only settlement by samurai outside of Japan. The group purchased land from the Charles Graner family in the Gold Hill region after coming to San Francisco in 1869. Though the group was able to successfully show their produce during the 1869 California State Agricultural Fair in Sacramento and the 1870 Horticultural Fair in San Francisco, the farm as a Japanese colony existed between 1869 and 1871.[11]

A third passage online gives a slightly different history of the Wakamatsu colony, reflecting the research of Japanese novelist Yoshio Takahashi whose 1983 book *Kaisho Suneru* (The Schnells from Overseas) contains his version of the Schnell brothers' history in Japan:

> Since John Henry was closely aligned with the Aizu-Wakamatsu clan (in Fukushima), the new Japanese colony near Sacramento was called the Wakamatsu Tea and Silk Colony. It was assumed that Schnell took people from Aizu-Wakamatsu to America, but Takahashi sensei believes that the settlers were mostly farmers from the Kanto area.[12]

These three passages give very conflicting information about the Wakamatsu colony expedition. The dates are accurate, but the information about the participants is problematical. The statement that the group consisted of twenty-two samurai and their families is unfounded. It is clear that the operation was organized and orchestrated by John Henry Schnell. His days as an arms dealer in Japan ended with the defeat of the Aizu domain at the hands of the new Meiji government. He gambled on a new career in the United States founded upon an enterprise producing two highly desired products—tea and silk—and he lost!

Schnell would have to hire skilled practitioners who knew a lot about producing tea and silk. He would also need carpenters and other workmen. When a local official arrived at the Wakamatsu farm to conduct the 1870 census, he listed about twenty-six names (including Schnell and his family) and their occupations. The list includes four carpenters and many others who are described as common laborers. Japanese samurai in the mid-nineteenth century held one of the highest ranks in Japanese society. They worked as local government officials and would not hold positions as carpenters or laborers. They had administrative skills, but rarely if ever performed such basic work as farming and carpentry. Schnell needed farmers and carpenters who were skilled at their crafts and who would work for low wages. So while he may have included one or more samurai in his group, they were likely the exception rather than the rule. There is, however, one Japanese settler who was perhaps a samurai. Matsunosuke Sakurai (c. 1834–1901) stayed on and worked for the Veerkamp family, who acquired the land in the 1870s and farmed it into the early years of the current century. He was the only one of the early colonists who stayed on at the Wakamatsu colony site after the death of Okei-san.

The first two passages state that the Japanese bought the land for the Wakamatsu farm from Charles Graner, but that is a misstatement. John Henry Schnell bought the land, and his name and his name alone is on the transfer of land agreement (see appendix II). The Japanese were workers employed by Schnell who had signed contracts in Japan that clearly specified that they were employees of Schnell with fixed salaries.

The Wikipedia passage states that the group consisted of twenty-two samurai and only one woman. There were indeed between twenty and twenty-five or more Japanese at the Wakamatsu farm, but the 1870 census list includes eight women (including Jou Schnell and her daughters) as well as a couple of adolescent girls. Several of the women were married and came with their husbands from Japan. Their ages varied greatly.

Then there is the assertion of Professor Takahashi that the group consisted of farmers from the Kanto (Tokyo) region of Japan and not from the Aizu area in northeast Japan. He is probably correct that the Japanese were farmers and not samurai, but it is hard to tell where they came from. There is no evidence where the workers came from, and there is no accurate list of who they were, what they did in Japan, and what occurred in their lives after the collapse of the Wakamatsu enterprise in California.[13]

There are reports that, with the defeat of the Aizu Domain, imperial troops captured John Henry Schnell and were going to arrest him. His pleas for mercy and his status as a foreigner won him his release on the condition that he immediately board a ship back to the foreign settlement in Yokohama. If this is the case, there was little time for him to recruit workers in Aizu for his California scheme. It would have been much easier for him to recruit workers in the Tokyo-Yokohama region, but any firm conclusion is hard to establish.

The Wakamatsu Colony Farm was a very bold endeavor. Remarkably, John Henry Schnell planned the whole project in a matter of months after the bitter defeat of the Aizu Domain in 1868. He decided on a destination, recruited a group of willing workers, assembled a large amount of supplies, and traveled to an alien land. After their arrival in California, Schnell bought a working farm, moved his group there, and began farming less than a month after their arrival in late May 1869. The colonists soon began cultivating tea plants, and there was some optimism that their venture might succeed.

THE LAND AND EARLY SETTLERS

The Gold Hill region is located in El Dorado County in east central California, about forty miles east of downtown Sacramento. It is a gently rolling plain of grassland, oaks, and seasonal streams located in the foothills of the Sierras, 1,200 feet above the Sacramento Valley. The soils are fertile, and water is available from two small creeks running through it. The region possesses a classic Mediterranean climate with cool rainy winters and hot and dry summers. The region is subject to periodic droughts, which can cause problems for farmers without dependable sources of water. It is only two miles away from Coloma, where James Marshall first discovered gold in 1848, and roughly six miles from Placerville.

Native Americans lived in this region for over six thousand years and continue to live throughout this area today. At the time of the Gold Rush, Gold Hill was inhabited by a people referred to by the name of their language, "Nisenan." The arrival of gold miners in 1848–1849 devastated the Nisenan people with disease and murder, but small numbers survived, and today the Nisenan language and culture are undergoing a strong revival with a younger generation that is proud of its heritage.

Because the Gold Hill area is so close to Coloma, when the word spread of possible gold throughout the region, large numbers of miners and prospectors with their claims, shacks, and tents covered the landscape. The settlement of Gold Hill quickly materialized not only for the extensive mining in the area, but also as a supply center for miners in need of supplies and food and drink. Later in the mid-1850s when most of the miners moved elsewhere, the population shrank and the main supply store eventually closed. The brick ruins of the store are visible to this day.

A group of four German families traveled together from Missouri to California in 1852. Among them were Charles Graner, Francis Veerkamp, his wife Louisa, and Louisa's sister Anna Fredricka Tobener. Anna and Charles married later that year, and the two families purchased separate ranches in the Gold Hill area. The Veerkamps settled at the foot of nearby Thompson Hill, while the Graners purchased 160 acres just north of Gold Hill (future home of the Wakamatsu Colony Farm) from an earlier owner, Sam Hill.

The Graners were active and successful farmers. They planted a large quantity of grape vines and also raised cattle, pigs, and sheep, as well as fruits and vegetables. When the grape vines matured, the Graners bottled wine and built a distillery for the production of brandy. Their alcoholic products were sold to miners seeking relief from the tedious work of prospecting. As the size of the Graner family grew, so did the size of their main farmhouse.

By 1868 when the gold frenzy was rapidly subsiding, the Graner family decided to sell the land and to move to San Francisco where they entered the hotel business. This was the point at which John Henry Schnell purchased the Graner farm and made it the site of the Wakamatsu Colony. Five years later, long after Schnell lost title to the land and had moved away, the Veerkamps purchased the property. Francis and his six sons did not continue the production of tea and silk. Instead, they raised fruit, grains, nuts, cattle, swine, and poultry.

The Veerkamps and their descendants continued to farm the land through the 1960s. The Coloma-based American River Conservancy purchased the land in November 2010 and is currently in the process of raising funds to protect the Wakamatsu Tea and Silk Colony farm's extensive natural and cultural history.[14]

METHODOLOGY OF RESEARCH

Very few scholars have attempted any studies of the Wakamatsu settlement. This is a serious omission since this colony was an important precursor to the massive immigration of tens of thousands of Japanese who began arriving in the 1880s. The most significant scholarly study is a chapter on the Wakamatsu colony by Professor John E. Van Sant in his 2000 book *Pacific Pioneers: Japanese Journeys to America and Hawaii, 1850–1880*.[15] Other important sources include Ikuo Torimoto's book, *Okina Kyū and the Politics of Early Japanese Immigration to the United States*,[16] and Paul Spickard's monograph, *Japanese Americans: The Formations and Transformations of an Ethnic Group*.[17] Other useful studies of East Asian immigration to the United States are

Ronald Takaki's *Strangers from a Different Shore: A History of Asian America*[18] and Erika Lee's *The Makings of Asian America: A History*.[19]

One factor inhibiting research is the sheer lack of original material. Neither Schnell, his family, nor his Japanese workers left any written records of their lives in California. We have no contemporary diaries, books, interviews, or other first-person materials. This lack of a written record leaves many holes concerning the main actors. The U.S. census of 1870 gives us a list of names of the Japanese present in early July 1870, but the census official mangled the Japanese names so badly that it is almost impossible to figure out who these people were.

Our main source for examining life at the Wakamatsu Colony comes from articles in contemporary local newspapers by journalists interested in learning something about these very alien people who suddenly appeared in their midst. Lengthy articles can be found in such contemporary publications as the *Daily Alta California*, the *Daily Morning Call*, The Placerville *Mountain Democrat*, the *Sacramento Daily Union*, and the *Pacific Rural Press*. Their coverage is extensive and quite detailed, providing key firsthand information about the colony. Unfortunately, we have to look at the colony through these journalists' untrained eyes. A great deal of their coverage comes from interviews with John Henry Schnell, who evidently spoke good English, but who was prone to exaggerate the success of the farm colony. The Japanese members of the colony, most of whom knew no English and in some cases may have been illiterate, remain totally silent.

There is one interesting source in German that purports to give the full story of John Henry's brother Edward Schnell in Japan.[20] Unfortunately a careful reading of the article reveals a very confused author. He combines the characters of Edward and John Henry Schnell into a single composite. Thus, in this account, it is Edward who befriends the leaders of the Aizu domain, who is made an honorary samurai, and who fights the imperial army. It is also Edward who gathers together a group of Japanese workers with some samurai who travel to California to set up the Wakamatsu farm. The author, Kurt Meissner, speculates that when "Edward" and his family left their California farm, they went on to Germany where Edward, who had served in the Prussian military prior to his arrival in Japan, served in the Franco-Prussian War (1870–1871). Meissner then has Edward back in Japan in 1872 and 1873. This statement we know is true, but it is apparent that there is little else that we can rely on in this article. Meissner's confusion in discerning between Edward and John Henry Schnell means that his work is fatally flawed.[21] Meissner says that he could not find much if anything about Edward Schnell in German sources and that Japanese sources are few and not terribly helpful. I agree with Meissner. There are a few Japanese articles about the Wakamatsu farm, but most of them are chock-full of errors and cannot be relied on.

It is said that there has been a renewed interest in Japan concerning the Japanese colonists who returned to Japan after the failure of the Wakamatsu Colony. Japanese researchers promise publications in the future that, when achieved, could provide fresh information for the next scholar who investigates the history of the settlement. I regret that I was unable to visit Japan yet again in my retirement to investigate this matter from a more Japanese perspective.

Even Okei Ito remains a deep mystery. Much has been written about her, but a great deal of that material is pure fiction. There is evidence that she did indeed come from the Aizu region. Yet, we know very little about her background, her brief life in California, and the circumstances surrounding her very premature death. The Veerkamp family, which took over the Wakamatsu Colony land by 1873, remembers her as a quiet, pretty, and lonely girl, but that is all.

The major source for the veneration of Okei-san by Japanese-American historians and novelists and movie producers in Japan is the work of Eiichiro Azuma, professor of history and Asian-American studies at the University of Pennsylvania. His book, *Between Two Empires: Race, History, and Transnationalism in Japanese America*,[22] and his book-length article, "'Pioneers of Overseas Japanese Development': Japanese American History and the Making of Expansionist Orthodoxy in Imperial Japan,"[23] clearly depict the use of the Okei-san legend by Japanese American historians and Japanese writers of the 1930s and early 1940s.

The chapter on Japan's Meiji Revolution and the Boshin Civil War of 1868–1869 relies on bountiful secondary source material available on the subject. One of the best sources is the late W. G. Beasley's 1972 book, *The Meiji Restoration*.[24]

The upshot is that we must rely on the words of contemporary journalists and little more. We can guess that some of the workers may have been samurai, for example, but we may never know for sure. The result is that the researcher will have to rely on guesswork at times and hope for the best.

NOTES

1. Personal interview with Margaret Mead, early 1971.
2. James L Huffman, *Down and Out in Late Meiji Japan* (Honolulu: University of Hawaii Press, 2018), 225.
3. Schnell's wife's name is sometimes reported as "Jou" or as "Oyoo."
4. American River Conservancy, *The Wakamatsu Tea & Silk Colony Farm: America's First Issei* (2012), 6.
5. Quoted in the *Mountain Democrat*, May 10, 2013.
6. John E. Van Sant, *Pacific Pioneers: Japanese Journeys to America and Hawaii, 1850–80* (Urbana and Chicago: University of Illinois Press, 2000), 129.
7. Van Sant, *Pacific Pioneers*, 130.
8. The *Daily Alta California*, a San Francisco newspaper that published between 1849 and 1891, is the main but by no means only source of news of the Wakamatsu colony in American

newspapers. Other newspapers providing coverage include The *Sacramento Daily Union,* the San Francisco *Daily Morning Call,* the Placerville *Mountain Democrat,* The San Francisco *Daily Evening Bulletin,* and the San Francisco *Pacific Rural Press.* Articles that announced the arrival of the Japanese (*Daily Alta California,* 5/27/1869) and the settlement of the Japanese (*Daily Alta California,* 6/16/1869) spread quickly to other newspapers across the country, which copied all of or parts of the original stories. They include the *Newark Advocate* (6/18/1869), the *Milwaukee Daily Sentinel* (6/30/1869), the *Morning Republican* (Arkansas 7/2/1869), the *Vermont Chronicle* (7/10/1869), *The Daily Cleveland Herald* (7/15/1869), and the *Weekly Georgia Telegraph* (7/16/1869).

9. Placerville *Mountain Democrat,* October 2, 1869.

10. The full application for the National Registry is to be found in appendix I of this text. The application provides a brief history of the Colony as well as very specific information about the buildings on the site and purchases made in the name of the colony which are not covered in great detail in the text of this book.

11. https://en.wikipedia.org/wiki/Wakamatsu_Tea_and_Silk_Farm_Colony. Accessed September 2, 2017.

12. http://photoguide.jp/log/2012/02/wakamatsu-tea-and-silk-farm-colony-at-gold-hill-california/. Accessed September 3, 2017. The writer of this blog is Philbert Ono

13. Several scholars in Japan have launched a search for the names and family histories of some of the Wakamatsu settlers, but they have not published their work to date.

14. Much of the information in this section is derived from the booklet *The Wakamatsu Tea & Silk Colony Farm*, published by the American River Conservancy.

15. Van Sant, *Pacific Pioneers.*

16. Ikuko Torimoto, *Okina Kyū and the Politics of Early Japanese Immigration to the United States* (Jefferson, NC: McFarland Publishing, 2016).

17. Paul Spickard, *Japanese Americans, The Formation and Transformation of an Ethnic Group* (New York: Twayne Publishing, 1996).

18. Ronald Takaki, *Strangers from a Different Shore: A History of Asian America* (New York: Back Bay Books, 1998).

19. Erika Lee, *The Making of Asian America: A History* (New York: Simon & Schuster, 2015).

20. Kurt Meissner, "General Eduard Schnell," *Monumenta Nipponica* 4, no. 2: (1941): 395–427.

21. See K. W. Lee, "Gold Hill Colony: Hope and Betrayal for a 'Mayflower,'" *Nichi Bei Times,* January 1, 2011.

22. Eiichiro Azuma, *Between Two Empires: Race, History, and Transnationalism in Japanese America* (New York: Oxford University Press, 2005).

23. Eiichiro Azuma, "'Pioneers of Overseas Japanese Development': Japanese American History and the Making of Expansionist Orthodoxy in Imperial Japan," *Journal of Asian Studies* 67, no. 4 (2008): 1187–1226.

24. W. G. Beasley, *The Meiji Restoration* (Stanford: Stanford University Press, 1972).

Chapter One

National Tension That Brought on the Boshin War in Japan and Refugees from the Aizu Domain to California

The Meiji Restoration of 1868 is generally seen in a very positive light, as Japan's impressive jump into the modern world and the start of its modern transformation. But there is a very dark side to this story. Even after the last Tokugawa shogun resigned his post and went away to live in retirement by early 1868, several domains in northeastern Honshu remained staunchly loyal to the shogunate and made it known that they would resist the new regime. The strongest resistance came from the Aizu domain with its proud military tradition. For this reason it was attacked in the fall of 1868 by the army of the new Meiji government which sought to spread its authority throughout Japan. Imperial troops, many of them from the western domains of Satsuma and Choshu which led the new regime, greatly outnumbered the small Aizu force. The imperial army began its attack of Aizu in October 1868 and, after a prolonged siege, burned Aizu's castle town of Wakamatsu to the ground and killed several thousand Aizu samurai and peasants who had taken refuge behind its walls. When Aizu finally surrendered in early November 1868, the Meiji government abolished the domain and forced many of its people into exile in a barren region in the far north. This destruction of their homeland convinced twenty to thirty of their residents to move to California in 1869 and 1870 to join a tea and silk farm colony at Gold Hill.

It is necessary at this stage to discuss the political crisis that engulfed Japan throughout the 1860s in order to explain why some Japanese came to California seeking new opportunities in 1869 even though it was still illegal for Japanese to leave their country without official permission until 1885. The coming of Western imperialism by the mid-nineteenth century led to the collapse of the Tokugawa shogunate (1600–1868) and to a military struggle between those Japanese loyal to the shogunate and other Japanese who wanted to create a strong modern government led by the Emperor that its adherents thought could better deal with the threats to the country's independence imposed by the West. This conflict led to the destruction of the Aizu *Han* or Domain[1] and the forced migration of its inhabitants to other regions of Japan.

Throughout its history Japan has gone through periods when it opened its doors to the outside world alternating with times when it chose national isolation. When Western explorers and traders from Spain, Portugal, Great Britain, Holland, and elsewhere began to venture to Japan in the later years of the sixteenth century through the start of the seventeenth century, some Japanese were initially quite welcoming. The Westerners sold guns and other items to the Japanese, and Christian missionaries made significant inroads in their efforts to convert many Japanese to their faith. Japanese armies invaded Korea, and Japanese traders sailed to China and Southeast Asia.

During this time Japan experienced a series of civil wars as various military groups vied for political supremacy. The ultimate victor was a military coalition led by Tokugawa Ieyasu, whose army won the decisive battle of Sekigahara in October 1600. The victors then created the Tokugawa Shogunate with its capital at Edo (now Tokyo) which effectively governed Japan until its collapse in 1867–1868.

Shortly after its inception the Tokugawa regime instituted an isolationist foreign policy (*Sakoku*—鎖国—"closed country") under which relations and trade between Japan and other countries were severely limited, nearly all foreigners were barred from entering Japan, and common Japanese people were prohibited from leaving the country.[2] The Tokugawa shogunate also banned the practice of Christianity. All foreign missionaries were obliged to leave Japan, and the active practice of the religion among Japanese was strictly forbidden.

The Tokugawa shogunate (*Bakufu*) governed Japan as a strict military dictatorship through to the middle years of the nineteenth century. Stable government and lasting peace contributed to the rapid growth of Japan's population and economy. There was a strong market economy with the beginnings of what later became banks and modern corporations such as Mitsui. There was the growth of large urban centers such as Edo and Osaka. The population was well-educated with high literacy rates for both men and women. By the time the American Navy, led by Commodore Matthew Perry, forced Japan to open its ports to Western commerce and relations in 1853 and 1854, Japan was a united nation with a strong economy and a well-educated population of over thirty million citizens.

The last decades of the Tokugawa Shogunate, however, found growing tensions throughout Japanese society. The leading elements of the merchant class were growing increasingly prosperous while many samurai, daimyo (domain governors), and the Shogunate itself were getting deeper into debt because their salaries and tax receipts remained constant year after year while inflation made their incomes worth less against increased expenses. The Tokugawa government had enforced a tight lid over Japanese society, but there was growing pressure throughout Japanese society that might someday lead to an explosion.[3] All that was needed was a catalyst to ignite a spark that would feed the fires of an explosive society.

The arrival of Commodore Matthew Perry and the American naval fleet in 1853 was that catalyst that led to rapid social change and to the collapse of the Shogunate. The Tokugawa government was in a quandary when faced with Perry's demands for open ports. It was well aware of the bitter defeat that China had experienced in the Opium War of 1839–1842. Five thousand British marines and sailors had destroyed much of China's coastal and river cities and thereby its shipping industry with relative impunity. The Japanese were wary of replicating China's defeat, but to give in to Perry's demands would expose the weakness of the shogunal government. The *Bakufu* decided the best course was to send out letters to many daimyo asking for their input, an effort which, if anything, further exposed its weakened position.[4]

The hesitation of the *Bakufu*, combined with the exposure to the threat of imperialism, precipitated a struggle between those desiring to maintain the status quo and those desiring change, culminated in the bitter Boshin War of 1868–1869. The battle was between forces loyal to the Tokugawa shogunate and "imperial forces" led by the domains of Satsuma and Choshu in far western Japan. They who hoped to create a strong central government, better able to protect Japan from the scourge of Western imperialism.

The forces fighting on the side of Satsuma and Choshu regarded the Tokugawa government as being too weak, corrupt, and inept to deal effectively with the Western powers that they perceived as threatening Japan's national independence. Their destruction of the pro-Tokugawa Aizu domain led directly to John Henry Schnell taking nearly thirty Aizu refugees with him to Gold Hill in California.

THE COLLAPSE OF THE SHOGUNATE

When Commodore Perry returned to Edo in 1854, the Japanese agreed to a treaty that opened several Japanese ports to American and later other European ships. By 1860, the United States and various European nations had negotiated trade agreements with the Tokugawa government which Emperor Komei refused to endorse. The very fact that the shogunate made these arrangements that allowed Westerners to enter Japan made it look hopelessly weak in the eyes of many Japanese. By the mid-1860s, the shogunate found its rule threatened from three directions. First, there was the pressure from Western powers that were eager to force Japan to open its doors. Second, there was a threat from more distant *tozama daimyo*[5] in such places as Satsuma and Choshu in western Japan. Finally, there was a risk of a rebellion by a group of young samurai known as *Shishi* or "men of purpose." Found more often in *tozama* domains such as Satsuma and Choshu, they called themselves "loyalists" who wanted to reinstate the emperor as the true ruler of Japan claiming that the *Bakufu* had usurped the emperor's position. Although they initially demanded the expulsion of all foreigners, some of their leaders such as Yoshida Shoin (1830–1859) developed a more pragmatic view of the West, stressing that Japan had to acquire the advanced technology of the West before it could gain true independence.

The mid-1860s saw growing military unrest against the *Bakufu*. By 1866, the domains of Satsuma and Choshu had agreed to a secret alliance against the shogunate. That year, fighters from Choshu defeated a force sent by the *Bakufu,* thus exposing its military weakness. The shogun, Tokugawa Yoshinobu (1837–1913), sought a compromise whereby he would return political authority to the emperor but where he would head a council of the daimyo. Unfortunately for him, the leaders of Satsuma and Choshu were determined to make a clean break from the past by overthrowing the old government by force. Their goal was the creation of a new strong government led by ambitious samurai who they thought would save Japan from the threats of the West. They promised to "restore" full authority to the Emperor who would nevertheless be under their control—hence, the term "Meiji Restoration." The new young Meiji Emperor was only fifteen years old at this time. On January 3, 1868, Satsuma and Choshu seized the imperial palace in Kyoto and proclaimed an "imperial restoration."[6]

Yoshinobu quietly retired to Osaka Castle, but some of his vassals in the Kansai region decided to keep fighting. They engaged imperial forces at Toba and Fushimi south of Kyoto, but the better trained and organized imperial troops, though outnumbered, won a resounding victory. Yoshinobu escaped by ship to Edo (now Tokyo) and hunkered down in his palace—now the imperial palace. Imperial troops marched to the outskirts of Edo where representatives of the imperial army met with officials serving the Shogun. They reached an agreement where the Shogun would surrender the city peacefully. Yoshinobu would be allowed to retire to peaceful exile in Mito (now Ibaraki Prefecture).

Although Yoshinobu had fully surrendered, resistance on his behalf continued. About two thousand shogunal troops gathered at a temple in what is now the Ueno district of Tokyo, but they were routed by a larger force of imperial troops. The war shifted to the north of the island of Honshu where several pro-shogunal domains formed an alliance under the leadership of the Aizu domain. Imperial troops marched north and engaged the allied domains at the battle of Aizu, which ended with the complete surrender of the Aizu city of Wakamatsu on November 6, 1868. There was further resistance in Hokkaido, but even those forces surrendered in early June 1869, bringing the whole country under the control of the new Meiji government.

THE ROLE OF AIZU'S DAIMYO MATSUDAIRA IN SUPPORT OF THE SHOGUNATE

Matsudaira Katamori (1836–1893), the *daimyō* or Lord of the Aizu domain who resided in the domain's main city, Wakamatsu, was one of a small group of *kamon daimyō*,[7] all of whom bore the Matsudaira name, but who in many cases were not directly related to the ruling Tokugawa family and thus not in line for the actual office of shogun. They served as loyal supporters of the Tokugawa clan. Since Kyoto, the home of the Japanese imperial court, was rapidly becoming the headquarters of the anti-shogunal movement, the *Bakufu* sought to counter this trend by restoring its powerbase in the old imperial capital. The Tokugawa government in Edo appointed Matsudaira, then twenty-six, as *shugoshoku*—defender of the shogunate—in the imperial capital. Historian Conrad Totman, author of *The Collapse of the Tokugawa Bakufu, 1862–1868*, explains that Matsudaira was chosen for this critical post because of Aizu domain's "tradition of stern warrior deportment and loyal service to Edo."[8]

Matsudaira proved to be an astute politician who attempted to keep the peace between the determined anti-*Bakufu* forces and the supporters of the Tokugawa government. The anti-Tokugawa coalition was still demanding that Japan return to its policy of national seclusion and the expulsion of all foreigners while the shogunate contended that increased contact and growing trade with the West was a regrettable necessity. Matsudaira himself criticized the shogunate's welcoming treatment of foreigners residing in Japan, but at the same time strongly opposed any move to return to national seclusion, recognizing that Japan was weak and only a modern and greatly strengthened Japan could resist the guns of the West.

Matsudaira tried hard to tread a very narrow road, hoping to gain support from both the shogunal and imperial forces in Kyoto. This middle-of-the-road policy was designed to bring some degree of "Court-*Bakufu* harmony." Unfortunately, this policy ultimately failed because relations between Matsudaira and the young ambitious samurai from Satsuma, Choshu, and other anti-shogunal domains were fraught with tension. Radical elements from Choshu became belligerent against the Aizu *daimyo* and his samurai warriors in Kyoto. The situation became so tense by 1864 that Matsudaira wanted to attack the Choshu forces camped on the outskirts of Kyoto, but the shogun refused to grant him permission. However, in 1865, Matsudaira and his forces participated in a shogunal raid against Choshu which forced the rebellious domain to temporarily pledge its allegiance to the shogun. But the shogun refused to allow Matsudaira to lead another raid on Choshu in 1866.

When the Shogun Tokugawa Yoshinobu resigned his post in late 1867, the ascendant armies of Satsuma and Choshu, which now fully controlled the imperial court and the youthful Meiji Emperor, later attacked the armies of Aizu and its allies in stressful battles in the outskirts of Kyoto, forcing Matsudaira and his surviving troops to retreat back to Aizu. Meanwhile, imperial forces were successful in winning control of Edo later in 1868. They renamed the city Tokyo and took control of the shogun's palace, which then became and still remains today the imperial palace. However, several domains such as Aizu remained loyal to the Tokugawa shogunate, even though the shogun had resigned. Although weakened by their battles in Kyoto, these domains decided to fight the new Meiji government, thus starting the civil conflict known as the Boshin War, which raged across Japan through 1868 and early 1869.

Historian Peter Duus states that prolonged resistance against the new Meiji government "was less inspired by traditional loyalty to the Tokugawa than by a fear at the new power acquired by the southwestern daimyo [of Choshu and Satsuma]. Provincial loyalty and sectionalism died harder than the authority of the Tokugawa, and fighting in the north did not end until six months after the fall of Edo."[9]

Matsudaira and his allies continued their fight despite the Shogun's resignation because it was not entirely clear at that time that the imperial forces actually controlled all of Japan. He and other northern *daimyo* maintained their loyalty to the Tokugawa shogunate, believing that the imperial forces had betrayed the legitimate government of Japan. Imperial forces knew that they could not rest easy until they had dealt with the pro-shogunal forces. They sent a large military force to attack Matsudaira's headquarters at Tsuruga Castle in the Aizu city of Wakamatsu.

Shogun Yoshinobu's surrender gave the imperial forces control of much of Japan including the Kansai and Kanto regions, but a coalition of domains north of Tokyo including Aizu determined to continue the resistance. The coalition included such domains as Sendai, Yonezawa, Shonai, and Nagaoka, as well as Aizu. Imperial troops moving north defeated coalition forces in Nagaoka in May 1868 before attacking and defeating a badly outnumbered Aizu army besieged at the castle at Aizu-Wakamatsu in October 1868.

The armies of the northern coalition included many able soldiers, but they were badly equipped and relied on more traditional fighting methods. The imperial troops that had created the new Meiji government in Tokyo had close ties with foreign arms dealers and received military assistance from some of the Western powers. As a result, their troops were better trained and well-armed. Because modern armaments were scarce, leaders of the northern coalition went so far as to create cannon out of wood reinforced with roping and firing stone projectiles. Unfortunately such cannon, installed on defensive structures, could only fire four or five projectiles before bursting. The daimyo of Nagaoka managed to procure two thousand modern French rifles and a couple of Gatling guns from German arms dealer John Henry Schnell. Despite this late influx of weapons, the imperial forces eventually overcame the daimyo of Nagaoka while John Henry Schnell moved his arms business to Aizu.

THE FALL OF THE AIZU HAN

Aizu's bitter defeat in the Boshin Civil War left the whole region in ruins and created the opportunity for John Henry Schnell to lead a group of Japanese to what they believed was going to be a new life in California in 1869. Conditions were so bad and prospects for the future so dire that leaving their homeland for a life in a new and very strange country was a viable option for some.

Aizu, located roughly one hundred miles north of Tokyo, lay deep in the mountains. It was unusually isolated, even for mountainous Japan. The rugged topography made travel and communication in and out of the domain a challenge. A person entering or leaving the domain had to scramble over high mountain passes on often primitive roads. When traveling through this region in the late 1960s, I had a sense of isolation—Tokyo was not so distant, but it may as well have been on a different planet. Travelers in earlier centuries had to contend not only with such wild creatures as bear and wild boar, but also had to fend off brigands who could work uncontested in this wild country. It is said that Aizu was a land unto itself, with a local dialect that was all but incomprehensible to the few outsiders who dared to enter the region.

As strong military supporters of the Tokugawa, Aizu was famous throughout Japan for its deep martial tradition and its very fierce loyalty to the shogunate. Aizu had a standing army which approached five thousand men in the mid-nineteenth century. Its code of conduct had such expressions as "Serve the shogun with single-minded devotion" and "Do not measure your loyalty by the standards of other domains." Other parts of the code also reflected this military tradition: "Do not neglect military readiness. . . . Do not confuse the duties of higher and lower ranks. . . . Older brothers should be respected and younger brothers loved. . . . Lawbreakers should not be treated with lenience. . . . The words of women should be totally disregarded." Any Aizu samurai was to comport himself with strict discipline at all times, avoiding all matters of personal pettiness.[10]

The Matsudaira clan established their seat of power in the old Aizu castle town of Wakamatsu, a strategically located hub in the center of the domain at the convergence of five major roads that crisscrossed northeastern Japan. The key fortification in Wakamatsu was Tsuruga Castle. Historian Janice P. Nimura writes:

> The graceful wing-like roof lines of Tsuruga Castle—*tsuru* means "crane"— belied its massive fortifications. Sheer walls twenty feet thick rose vertically from the moats, each massive block of stone bearing the chisel marks of the laborers who had wrestled it into place centuries earlier. In places, the drop from the top of the wall to the algae-green surface of the moat was fifty feet. On the inside, the walls were a maze of stone steps, some flights broad enough for fifteen men to run straight up towards the outer edge; others, barely wide enough for one, tracing diagonal paths up and down at intervals. The castle itself rested on a stone foundation two stories high.[11]

The new imperial government sent a large army to northern Japan in the summer and fall of 1868 to conquer the northern domains such as Aizu which remained loyal to the Tokugawa shogunate despite the fact that the sitting shogun had in fact surrendered to the new government months earlier. The imperial army had modern guns and cannons purchased from a coterie of Western arms dealers. It had close to seventy-five thousand soldiers drawn from thirty-four domains. Aizu on the other hand had a far smaller force including four thousand peasants, nearly three thousand samurai, and four hundred elderly warriors.[12]

Writer Mariko Nagai of Temple University, Japan describes the fighting that took place in and around the castle as imperial troops laid siege and gradually wore down the Aizu samurai defenders inside. She asks us to remember the Byakko-tai whose fate became part of Japan's military lore:

> A group of 13- to 17-year old boys formed the Byakko-tai (White Tiger Unit) to defend the only path leading to Tsuruga Castle, but they were only armed with ancient rifles and swords. When they saw smoke coming from their castle, they committed suicide rather than having to live in shame and loss.
>
> Knowing that their men would not be able to fight if they had to worry about their families, many women killed their children and committed suicide. Probably the most well-known woman warrior was Yae Yamamoto, who fought as a sniper in the besieged castle during the month of bombardment with cannons and rifles. According to one source, during nearly 30 days of siege, 2,500 cannon balls on average were shot into the castle. With people dying, injuries, and food and water supplies running short, Yae ran around eliminating enemies. Whenever cannon balls dropped near them, other clan women would hug the explosives in their arms with blankets, sometimes blowing themselves up while trying to defuse them. . . . Those who survived were labeled traitors and became fugitives hiding out in the mountains. By all accounts, this was one of the bloodiest and most brutal of wars.[13]

The most serious fighting of the Boshin War came to an end in November 1868 when imperial forces crushed the resistance inside Tsuruga Castle. The imperial forces led by Satsuma and Choshu had had ample funds to purchase advanced weaponry including Minié rifles and shell-firing cannon from foreign arms dealers. Aizu, on the other hand, had very little in the way of modern weapons beyond what they had bought from the Schnell brothers. Their resources were low, the financial situation grim, and the samurai army largely untrained despite the last-minute training afforded them by Schnell. Their overall situation was desperate compared to the well-armed and well-trained imperial army that was poised to destroy the last effective resistance to their cause.

The people of Aizu suffered terrible casualties at the hands of the imperial army. There was a high rate of suicides. Diana E. Wright notes that "the Meiji regime's proclamation of a scorched-earth policy in regards to the 'eastern rebels,' combined with rumours of an imperial army plan to slaughter all Aizu males and sell Aizu women to 'Occidentals,' made death an appealing alternative to capture. Indeed, it was a given that, to paraphrase Mao, war is not a tea ceremony."[14] The combined Aizu soldier death toll from its struggle against Choshu and Satsuma forces rose to nearly three thousand. Nearly five thousand survivors were taken prisoner, many of whom were forced to relocate from Aizu for Tanami, a cold barren region at the northern tip of Honshu.[15]

The imperial forces arrested the Aizu daimyo Matsudaira Katamori, seized his assets, and sentenced him to death, but after some time under house arrest in Tokyo, his life was spared because the new Meiji government needed popular support. Killing Matsudaira would make him a martyr in the eyes of his followers. He retired from active life and became the Chief Priest of the Nikko Toshogu Shrine, a memorial to the founder of the Tokugawa shogunate. He held this position until his death on December 5, 1893.[16]

Defeat turned the world of the people of Aizu into a living hell. Their homes and land lay in ruin. They lived in bare camps that were exposed to all the elements of northern Japan's rough winter weather. Many residents of Wakamatsu were forced to leave the terrible wreckage of their city and their farm land for nearby prison camps. Many were filthy and covered with lice. The proud sturdy old world they had previously known was gone forever.[17]

The new Meiji government took direct control of the domain's affairs. Sadly, according to historian Marius Jansen, "no other domain was treated as harshly" as Aizu in the aftermath of the civil war.[18] After a year of indecision, the new Meiji government forced the people of Aizu to leave their homeland and to move north to the tip of Honshu, a wild and desolate land, in the newly created province of Tonami.[19] Others went to barren Hokkaido to start a new life. The Meiji government chartered American ships to ferry them to the north in the spring of 1869. Conditions were not so bad in summer, but starting in late autumn the desperation of their situation became very clear—not enough rice, no proper shelter, and a lack of warm clothes in this very northern climate. Janice Nimura writes:

> Supplies of firewood ran out. Porridge froze solid in the pot. The settlers dug for the roots of bracken under the snow, collected the seaweed that washed up on the shore, and tried to make the meager stores of soybeans and potatoes last. The lucky ones ate dog meat.[20]

A handful of these unfortunate Aizu residents would soon travel to Coloma, California, to set up a colony in a new land that they heard was brimming with incredible wealth.

REMEMBERING AIZU: THE TESTAMENT OF SHIBA GORŌ

There are few contemporary accounts of the vast suffering the people of Aizu as a result of the new Meiji government's decision to quash all resistance to its rule. One can gain some understanding through the eyes of Shiba Gorō (1859–1945) who was born into an Aizu samurai family. At the age of ten he was an eyewitness to the savagery of the attack of the large imperial army in October and November 1868. Shiba lost several close members of his family including his mother and grandmother who both committed suicide. When Aizu surrendered, he, his surviving family, and many Aizu folk were first taken as prisoners to Tokyo and were later exiled to northern Honshu where he lived with his father on the edge of starvation.

Shiba survived the cruel life in exile and after a few years was able to make his way back to Tokyo. After working as a house servant for a time, he gained admittance to a military school run by the Meiji government in Tokyo. Government authorities soon recognized his intelligence and willingness to work hard. After graduation he swiftly rose through the ranks to become a full general. Shiba saw action in the Sino-Japanese War (1894–1895) and the Russo-Japanese War (1904–1905) and became military attaché at the Japanese embassy in Beijing at the time of the Boxer rebellion of 1900. Shiba won many accolades from Japanese and foreign officials for the astute manner in which he organized the defense of the embassies during the rebellion.

Nobody knows for sure when Shiba wrote the manuscript for *Remembering Aizu*, but it was certainly completed by 1942. Chūō kōronsha published a Japanese version in 1971 and the University of Hawaii Press published an English version in 1999 with Teruko Craig as the translator.[21]

Shiba explains that Aizu's motivation to fight the imperial army was not only its profound loyalty to the Tokugawa shogunate, but also its sentiment that the Restoration had been a coup led by a few Western domains—notably Satsuma and Choshu—that had little national backing as well as its belief that the Tokugawa were the legitimate rulers of Japan. But he goes even further, saying that Aizu reconciled itself to the new government but despite this move, the Meiji government branded "Aizu an enemy of the court—a rebel domain—and the entire populace was subjected to unspeakable abuses. The memory haunts me still."[22]

> Some historians who have written about the war have portrayed Aizu as the ringleader of those who wanted to preserve the feudal order at any cost. These historians have seen Satsuma and Choshu as the forces of liberation; supposedly, Aizu peasants and townsmen welcomed them and even gave them their active cooperation. This is a great distortion of the facts. There are countless documents that attest to the atrocities the enemy perpetrated on these very people, or for that matter, on common people throughout the northeastern domains. To my deep regret, these accounts have all been deliberately suppressed.[23]

Shiba goes to great length to show how the imperial army totally destroyed the castle and the town of Wakamatsu until the entire domain had become a wasteland. They are scoundrels "who think nothing of killing womenfolk of townsmen and peasants. They even leave the corpses of women strewn along the streets. . . . The castle precincts have been reduced to ashes. There isn't a thing left. Most of the houses in the city have been burned down. The commoner women who were captured have been sent to work as servants. There has been talk of violence and heinous deeds. . . . The castle reminded me of a wounded warrior struggling to get to his feet. It was piteous to behold, an utterly heartbreaking sight.[24]

When the fighting was over, the whole domain lay in ruins. The people of Aizu were forced to leave Aizu moving north to a frigid volcanic zone with soil so porous it was impossible to live well. Their lives in ruins, it is not surprising that at least a handful of the survivors would be willing to move to California. Shiba describes the scene of families taking the agonizing hike from Aizu into exile:

> Thinking back on it we must have looked like a procession of beggars: men with arms in slings, others limping on crutches, still others struggling to keep up but gradually falling behind, and not least of all, the grey-haired elderly carried piggyback by their attendants. We walked in complete silence, each burdened with his own fate. We had not the faintest inkling of what lay ahead and would slog on as our strength held out.[25]

Exile was miserable in the cold barren land of what is now Aomori prefecture. The Aizu survivors struggled to survive for a few years before tensions and memories eased and some made their way back home.

Chapter 1

NOTES

1. During the Edo/Tokugawa period of Japanese history (1600–1868), Japan was divided up into roughly three hundred political units known as domains (*Han*) administered by *daimyo* (lords) and their samurai retainers. The samurai class, including wives and children, accounted for 5 to 6 percent of the entire population of approximately thirty million Japanese in the early nineteenth century. See W. G. Beasley, *The Meiji Restoration* (Stanford: Stanford University Press, 1972), 24.

2. The Tokugawa government never used the term "sakoku." Instead, it's a word used by modern scholars to describe a series of regulations issued by the new government in the 1630s. *Sakoku* ("closed country") was the extreme isolationist foreign policy of the Japanese Tokugawa shogunate, which greatly limited relations and trade between other countries and Japan. Virtually all foreigners were excluded from entering Japan, and most Japanese were forbidden to leave their homeland. This policy was enacted in the 1630s and remained in force until 1854 when the American navy led by Commodore Matthew Perry forced Japan to open three ports. Holland was the only Western nation allowed limited access to Japan for trade during the Edo period (1600–1868).

3. There was a Japanese emperor on the throne throughout this period, but he was at best a weak figurehead in Kyoto. Emperor Komei (reigned 1846–1867) ruled with a much stronger hand than usual and caused great difficulties for the Tokugawa regime.

4. The Convention of Kanagawa, signed under threat of force by the Americans, effectively meant the end of Japan's 220-year-old policy of national seclusion by opening the ports of Shimoda and Hakodate to American vessels. It also ensured the safety of American castaways and established the position of an American consul in Japan. The treaty also precipitated the signing of similar treaties establishing diplomatic relations with other Western powers.

5. A *tozama daimyo* was a daimyo (territorial lord) who was considered an outsider by the rulers of Japan. The term was commonly used during the Edo period (1600–1868).

6. The reign of the Meiji Emperor (1868–1912) is known as the "Meiji Period." During this time the Japanese transformed themselves from a weak isolated island nation into a major world industrial and military power.

7. Houses whose lords were collaterals of the Tokugawa and bore the family name Matsudaira. *Kamon daimyo* were members of the manifold branches of the Tokugawa family, whether they bore the Tokugawa name or the much earlier Matsudaira surname.

8. Conrad Totman, *The Collapse of the Tokugawa Bakufu* (Honolulu: University of Hawaii Press, 1980), 227.

9. Peter Duus, *The Rise of Modern Japan* (New York: Houghton Mifflin, 1976), 72.

10. Janice Nimura, *Daughters of the Samurai: A Journey from East to West and Back* (New York: W. W. Norton, 2015), chapter 2.

11. Nimura, *Daughters*, chapter 2.

12. Diana E Wright, "Female Combatants and Japan's Meiji Restoration: The Case of Aizu," *War in History* 8, no. 4 (2001): 400.

13. Mariko Nagai, "And They Crossed the Ocean," *Wakamatsu Farm News*, Spring 2017, 1.

14. Wright, "Female Combatants," 405.

15. Wright, "Female Combatants," 410–15.

16. Van Sant writes: "Satsuma and Choshu had condemned Matsudaira to death before the battles of Toba and Fushimi but, surprisingly, he was spared. He and Tokugawa Yoshinobu were formally pardoned in a decree issued the following year. Charles De Long, who replaced Van Valkenberg as the U.S. minister to Japan, believed that the new government, well aware of its precarious control over Japan, feared that their deaths by execution or ritual suicide would have the 'inevitable consequences' of elevating them to martyrdom and acting as a unifying symbol to daimyos still incensed at their defeat." John E. Van Sant, *Pacific Pioneers: Japanese Journeys to America and Hawaii, 1850–80* (Urbana and Chicago: University of Illinois Press, 2000), 121–22.

17. Nimura, *Daughters*, chapter 2.

18. Quoted in Van Sant, *Pacific Pioneers*, 122.

19. Now Toyama Prefecture.

20. Nimura, *Daughters*, 122.
21. Shiba Gorō, *Remembering Aizu: The Testament of Shiba Gorō* (Honolulu: University of Hawaii Press, 1999).
22. Shiba, *Remembering Aizu*, 28.
23. Shiba, *Remembering Aizu*, 45.
24. Shiba, *Remembering Aizu*, 55–62.
25. Shiba, *Remembering Aizu*, 67.

Chapter Two

John Henry Schnell's Service to the Aizu Domain and His Decision to Move to California

John Henry Schnell probably conceived the idea of creating the Wakamatsu farm in California only after the demise of the Aizu Domain. Exactly when and how he came to that conclusion is only one of many mysteries in his elusive life. Even today we know next to nothing about his youth, his decision to come to Japan, how he became involved with the military defense of Aizu Wakamatsu, why and how he planned the Wakamatsu colony in Gold Hill near Coloma, California, and what happened to him and his family after their mysterious departure from the farm in June 1871. He remains one of the most shadowy persons in Japan at the start of the Meiji period.

It seems probable that John Henry and his younger brother Edward were possibly originally from Baden-Württemburg in what is now southwest Germany. John Henry was born in the early 1840s, probably around 1841, although some sources date his birth as late as 1843.[1] By 1860 the word began to spread throughout the United States and much of Europe that Japan was opening its formerly closed doors to the West and that Westerners seeking to enhance their fortunes might have some success there. John Henry and Edward arrived in Japan at some point in the very early 1860s. John Henry found employment for a brief time in the Prussian Legation in Tokyo while Edward did the same for the Dutch legation.

Although we do not know much about the origins of the Schnell brothers, some sources provide suggestions about their younger years. Apparently Edward had served in the Prussian Army in the 1850s, had some military expertise, and knew a lot about weapons of that period. He may have spent some time in Southeast Asia at some point because it is said that he had a spoken knowledge of Malay. He must have arrived in Japan no later than 1862 as he had a seven-year-old child from his Japanese wife Kawaii Tsugonusuke in 1869. He is also listed as owner of Plot "No. 44" in Yokohama. John Henry, who probably arrived in Japan around the same time, served as secretary and translator to the Prussian diplomat Max von Brandt[2] in the early 1860s.[3]

Whatever their reasons for traveling to Japan, the brothers did not have an easy time. Once while traveling through Edo in an open coach in 1867, Edward and John Henry Schnell barely survived an attack by a fanatical anti-foreign samurai from Numata. The samurai was a strong supporter of the nativist *Sonnō jōi* ("Revere the Emperor, Expel the Barbarians") movement. The attacker drew his sword, but was shot in the chest and forced to flee before he could inflict any real harm on the Schnells. Max von Brandt filed a complaint with shogunal authorities demanding that they punish the attacker, but no action was taken by the Japanese who probably came to the conclusion that the attacker had been punished enough because of his wounds. Oddly, the bodyguards provided by the Tokugawa Shogunate just stood by during the attack doing nothing to defend their Western guests.[4]

Both John Henry and Edward also sought other lines of work to enhance their fortune. There was already a ready market in the United States and Europe for Japanese cultural products, and the Schnell brothers were quick to collect lacquerware and perhaps other goods for export to Europe. They also sold world maps in Japan at a time when few Japanese had any real idea of world geography. But their main business—a form of work common to many foreigners in Japan at the time—was in importing and selling weapons and munitions to interested parties in Japan. One of their best customers was Daimyo Matsudaira of Aizu.[5]

By 1867 and 1868, at the time of the Boshin War, John Henry and his brother Edward were very much involved in the arms trade, selling arms probably from American and European sources.[6] Their status as weapons dealers made them especially attractive to at least some of the protagonists in the civil war. The triumphant imperial forces procured ample supplies of weapons from Western dealers, while a smaller group, which included the Schnell brothers, made good money selling guns and ammunition to members of the anti-imperial Northern Coalition, which included Aizu.

According to Professor Ikuko Torimoto, author of the recent monograph *Okina Kyūin and the Politics of Early Japanese Immigration to the United States, 1868–1924*,[7] when the last strong resistance against the imperial forces came from the coalition pro-Tokugawa domains in the northeastern Tōhoku region of the island of Honshu, foreign merchants including the Schnell brothers raced to the port of Niigata to sell weapons to the Alliance. Agents from the Yonezawa Domain ordered two thousand modern French-made rifles and three Gatling guns, foreign-made rifles, 250 seven-shot revolvers, ammunition, and a detonator from the Schnells in Yokohama in late April or early May 1868. The Schnells sent the weapons by ship, carefully avoiding forces loyal to the imperial army by going north around the tip of Honshu and then down to the port of Niigata on the Sea of Japan. Edward Schnell arrived with this cargo on May 12, sixteen days before John Henry Schnell arrived in Niigata.[8]

Reportedly, the Schnell brothers not only provided weapons, they also taught the Japanese how to use them. The *Ochikochi Shimbun* (newspaper) of July 1868 noted that "two Prussians came to Aizu where they provided training for the three types of military units and manufacturing of devices. Furthermore, because they opened up gold and silver mines, it is said that they serve at Wakamatsu Castle and utilize much of Aizu's transactions of the gold and silver circulating in the vicinity of Kosagoe."[9]

According to Japanese histories of the Aizu-Wakamatsu region, Kawa Tsuginosuke, a chief retainer of the northern Nagaoka Domain, had at an earlier time introduced John Henry to the leaders of the Aizu Domain, which had to replace weapons lost during the earlier Battle of Toba-Fushimi. On March 23, 1868, the Aizu Domain purchased weaponry totaling $15,000 including 780 rifles from John Henry. These weapons were also secretly piled onto a ship in Yokohama and transported to Niigata, where they were offloaded and sent to Wakamatsu. When John Henry himself arrived at the Aizu Domain, he developed close relations with the Domain's leaders. They built him a comfortable house to live in, made him an honorary samurai with the name Hiramatsu (with the same two *kanji* characters as in Matsudaira's name), and allowed him to marry the daughter of a local samurai. Her name was Jou.[10] John Henry trained Matsudaira's samurai in the use of modern guns and was placed in charge of a unit of Aizu samurai during the latter part of the Boshin War.[11]

One contemporary Japanese writer recorded the following observations of Schnell:

> Schnell is a merchant who sells weapons to the Tōhoku army.[12] I wonder why he gained the trust of the Aizu clan. . . . Also, the Schnell who came to supervise the setting up of big cannons, I heard that he did not have much experience with the big cannons, but he was wearing a big helmet with a *three-Aoi* (Tokugawa) crest, wearing a *Bussaki-Haori,* a Japanese half-coat, an outdoor damask (*Hakama*) and shoes. He appeared to be a distinguished supervisor. However, his Japanese was good.[13]

The Meiji government was well aware that Schnell had led Aizu and Northern Alliance troops against its army. When the fighting came to an end, Schnell was captured and was about to be arrested when he bowed his head and begged for mercy. Being a foreigner, he was quickly released and soon left by ship from Niigata to Yokohama with the promise that he would soon leave Japan.[14] It is unclear how quickly he left for California and whether he recruited Japanese workers from Aizu or from the Kanto region surrounding Tokyo and Yokohama or from both regions.

The identity of the Japanese colonists is a real mystery. We know the names of only a few of the workers and we do not know where they came from. There are, however, some hints. We know that the young Okei Ito came from Aizu and that she crossed the Pacific with a group of eight to ten other colonists. It is far more likely that she would have traveled with a group from the Aizu region than with a group of strangers from elsewhere. We also know that Schnell brought an Aizu banner with him, an act that would have been odd if the workers were not from Aizu. Finally, when Schnell landed in San Francisco, he made reference to the possibility that the former *daimyo* Matsudaira might come someday—something that might happen only if the colony had Aizu people. Therefore, it is the assumption in this study that the workers were from Aizu even though there is no concrete proof.

We do not know the whereabouts of John Henry, his wife, and two baby daughters after they left Coloma in June 1871. We do know that Edward Schnell stayed in Japan until at least 1872 or 1873, when he reached several financial settlements with the new Meiji government in Tokyo. What eventually became of the Schnell brothers is not certain even today. Rumors abound including some who say that John Henry did return to Japan but was executed and that Edward was supposedly seen in Switzerland in the 1880s. One wonders if this mystery will ever be solved.

A DECISION TO MOVE TO CALIFORNIA

The destruction of Aizu Wakamatsu most probably convinced John Henry Schnell that he and his new family had no future in Japan. Because of the active role that he had played in procuring weapons for Aizu and in fighting with Aizu samurai against the imperial army, he probably concluded that it would be better for him to take his family and to leave the country for new opportunities.

It is unclear how or when John Henry Schnell conceived of setting out to California. He could easily have escaped Japan with his wife and daughter, but he devoted much attention to the idea of taking a number of Japanese with him to create a Japanese settlement there. Schnell's plan was carefully and meticulously thought out. He decided to focus on the production of tea and silk, hired Japanese workers who understood the production of these goods, and bought a large quantity of seedlings and tools to develop his farm. He may have conceived of going elsewhere, perhaps to Australia, but at that time a future in California was on the minds of many adventurous men around the world.

Professor Van Sant writes:

> Since the new government in Japan was well aware of Schnell's direct support of their main enemy, his future prospects were limited. With Matsudaira's support, Schnell devised a plan to establish a colony of Aizu settlers in California that would produce tea and silk. Such a venture would be profitable for Aizu, which had lost most of its land to the central government as a result of the civil war.[15]

There is no doubt that Schnell's California planning came after Aizu's defeat, but there is no hard evidence that the former Daimyo Matsudaira was involved in the planning process and that he gave his "consent" to the project. Imperial forces imprisoned the Aizu chieftain immediately after his surrender and confiscated his wealth. There is no record of Matsudaira meeting with Schnell after the fighting stopped.

There is also no record of either of the Schnells visiting California before 1868 and no indication that Edward Schnell ever went there. California's fame came as a result of the recent gold rush, but by then there was the realization in California that the future of the local economy rested on agriculture and not gold mining. Newspapers worldwide talked of the mad rush for gold, but Schnell never thought seriously about prospecting gold. He most likely heard that the state of California was paying generous bounties to those people endeavoring to get involved in the production of silk and tea.

One must wonder, however, how much John Henry Schnell knew about California's soil and climate. Northern Japan has a warm, wet climate in summer and a long snowy winter, but that is not the case in northern California. There is a strong Mediterranean climate in much of California with hot dry summers and cool and often rainy winters in the foothills of the Sierra Nevada Mountains. Japan rarely experiences prolonged periods of drought, but as recent years have taught us, California is often a victim of severe droughts and unusual weather.

THE LEADERSHIP OF JOHN HENRY SCHNELL

John Henry Schnell was the sole creator and leader of the Wakamatsu Colony from start to finish. There is no evidence that Schnell collaborated with any Japanese officials while making plans to move to California. Schnell, and Schnell alone, appears to have conceived of the plan and to have executed it on his own. He drew up labor contracts in Japan with Japanese workers he wished to bring with him. The workers were responsible only to Schnell and not to any other corporation or group. This fact is substantiated by a news report in the San Francisco–based *Daily Morning Call* dated January 1, 1870.[16]

> The arrival and settlement of Herr Schnell and his Japanese, commonly known as the Japanese colony, has given new impetus to vinicultural pursuits. They had never before appreciated the value of the land, or been aware of its adaptability which is now being put, but the knowledge and experience of Herr Schnell has convinced them that their soil is of great value and with proper cultivation will yield handsome returns.
>
> And let me correct here an erroneous impression that has gained general credence. That is, that the Japanese have come here of their own accord to settle and establish a community and that Herr Schnell is their agent. Such is not the case. The enterprise is a private speculation of Mr. Schnell's. He has purchased the land, cultivates it upon his "own hook," and simply hires the Japanese, paying them regular monthly wages, under contracts made in Japan, and the honors and profits, as well as the drawbacks, are Schnell's alone. He has now twenty-one Japanese [17] in his employ comprising seven women and fourteen men; this number may be amply sufficient for all the land he can successfully cultivate for some time, and he will only send for more as he may require them. The success of his enterprise will not bring any Japanese here of their own accord, except such as he may desire to hire for wages, or unless others, taking advantage of his success, conclude to embark in the same business, so that all the hopes or fears of a large Japanese immigration to spring from this experiment may as well be at once dismissed.

There is also no explanation of how Schnell got his Japanese out of a Japan that strictly prohibited emigration. Did he smuggle them on to the ship leaving for San Francisco? Did he bribe Japanese officials to let them board? One report in the California *Mountain Democrat of* October 2, 1869, had duplicates of passports used by Japanese authorities "whereby large numbers of males and females designed to join" have been detained in Japan. It is unclear what this all means. Did Schnell use these duplicate passports to get his Japanese workers aboard this and later ships? Did the fact that he could only bring six Japanese with him mean that others were detained? Were those detained later somehow able to leave? We have no answers to these questions.

Some scholars have wondered whether the Japanese workers were genuine refugees or, instead, indentured workers like those who went to Hawaii a year earlier. The situation is ambiguous, but most if not all the indentured workers in Hawaii most likely had every intention of returning to Japan in the near future while the Wakamatsu workers had every intention of staying in the United States on a more permanent basis. They had signed contracts with Schnell but were free to leave at will, which is exactly what happened. It is in this sense that the Wakamatsu settlement was a true colony.

NOTES

1. The 1870 Federal Census lists John Henry Schnell as a farmer aged twenty-nine living in Coloma, California. The same census, dated July 1, 1870, also lists his wife, a Japanese

national aged twenty-four and their two daughters, Frances, aged two and her younger sister Mary aged two months. Data retrieved from ancestry.com.

2. Max von Brandt (1835–1920) had a long and distinguished career as a German diplomat in Japan and China. He was also a respected scholar in the field of Asian studies.

3. John E. Van Sant, *Pacific Pioneers: Japanese Journeys to America and Hawaii, 1850–80* (Urbana and Chicago: University of Illinois Press, 2000), 123–24.

4. See *The London and China Telegraph*, November 6, 1867, 578.

5. Van Sant, *Pacific Pioneers*, 123. The actual source of their weaponry is not entirely clear. Some historians speculate that many of the weapons were procured from the United States after the end of the American Civil War.

6. There was a large surplus of guns in the United States due to the recent Civil War.

7. Ikuko Torimoto, *Okina Kyūin and the Politics of Early Japanese Immigration to the United States, 1868–1924* (Jefferson, NC: McFarland Publishing, 2016), chapter 4.

8. Torimoto, *Okina Kyūin*, chapter 4.

9. Sven Saaler and Kudo Akira, eds., *Mutual Perceptions and Images in Japanese-German Relations* (Leiden: Brill, 2017), 122.

10. We know very little about John Henry Schnell's wife. There is the presumption that she was the daughter of a samurai. Most sources state that her name was Jou, but a few state she was known as "Oyoo." We do not know the date of her marriage to Schnell nor the circumstances that led to the marriage.

11. Torimoto, *Okina Kyūin*, chapter 4.

12. The Tōhoku army were the forces of the northern coalition.

13. Torimoto, *Okina Kyūin*, chapter 4.

14. Saaler and Akira, *Mutual Perceptions*, 129.

15. Van Sant, *Pacific Pioneers*, 123.

16. "Up in El Dorado" in the *Daily Morning Call*, January 1, 1870.

17. A few more Japanese came later, probably during the summer of 1870.

Chapter Three

Japanese Immigration to the United States

By 1869, tens of thousands of Chinese had emigrated to California and other parts of the United States in the late 1800s. They were part of the great diaspora of Chinese during the second half of the nineteenth century not only to North America but also to Hawaii, Australia, South America, and in greatest numbers to Southeast Asia. They went abroad to escape the chaos that accompanied the decline of the Qing dynasty (1644–1911), which included the disastrous Taiping Rebellion (1850–1864) that killed perhaps as many as twenty million Chinese and devastated the Chinese economy as well as the Opium Wars and other deadly rebellions.

The Chinese began arriving in California as early as 1849. They came as miners, but when the mines were depleted, they went on to other work in agriculture and in railway construction. The Coloma-Gold Hill region attracted many Chinese miners soon after James Marshall's discovery, but by the time Schnell and his Japanese workers came, the mines in the region were largely depleted and most of these Chinese immigrants had gone elsewhere.

White Californians treated the Chinese badly. The Chinese faced severe discrimination and were often badly beaten by white ruffians. They could not own land, were greatly restricted in terms of what occupations they could enter, and were severely criticized for taking jobs that paid them far less than what white men would receive for the same kind of work. Their determination to continue their struggle meant that they would survive as a community. Returning to China was not a good option for many as conditions worsened there.

The Wakamatsu Japanese, on the other hand, received a very warm welcome from white Californians. They were praised for their polite manners, hard work ethic, and great discipline. They were accepted as contributing members of California society who offered no threat to the job or economic security of white America. Based on many favorable newspaper articles written about the colonists, it's fair to say that these feelings lasted throughout their two years at Gold Hill.

Unfortunately, these good feelings only lasted when there were only a few Japanese in North America. When the Japanese revised rules concerning emigration in 1885, there was a flood of Japanese coming to North America—over a hundred thousand by the early 1900s. The reaction of many white Americans to this new influx of immigrants was harsh and often violent. The good feelings that had welcomed the Wakamatsu Japanese were long gone, and the amiable relations between Japan and the United States that had existed since the start of the Meiji era began to decline, culminating in war at Pearl Harbor.

There are two distinct eras that marked Japanese immigration to the United States. The earlier "frontier era" saw small groups of Japanese immigrants starting with those who came with Schnell in 1869. This earlier period of U.S.–Japanese relations was generally amicable. Although there were isolated acts of overt racism inflicted on Japanese, the evidence shows that racial discrimination against Japanese was not the norm. Only after large numbers of Japanese began to immigrate after 1885 did the tide of racism against Japanese begin to turn.

The Japanese who arrived in San Francisco in May 1869 left their country because of the vast destruction of their homeland as a result of the Boshin War. Unlike individual or small groups of Japanese who came in the "frontier era," they were genuine pioneers. Americans viewed them as members of a hardworking "model minority" when comparing them to the much-despised Chinese. John Van Sant correctly notes that "the agricultural goods they brought with them from Japan and their construction of a silk and tea farm indicated that they planned to remain in America for a long time, perhaps permanently." In this sense they were more representative of the Japanese farmers and laborers who began to emigrate to America and Hawaii in the late 1800s.[1]

JAPANESE IMMIGRATION

Ethnic Japanese have played a critical role in American history. They were the largest ethnic Asian group in the United States for most of the twentieth century. Waves of Japanese began emigrating in the mid-1880s through the mid-1920s. There were scattered Japanese settlements throughout the United States, but the largest concentrations lived in California. First-generation Japanese (*Issei*) initially worked as farm laborers or for the railroads, but many of them, as well as second-generation Japanese (*Nisei*), became farmers themselves or worked in a wide variety of other fields. Many Japanese came as *dekaseginin* or "workers away from home" who planned to save enough money abroad before returning home with their savings. While many did return to Japan, a high percentage decided to remain in the United States or Hawaii, often to establish their own farms and businesses. Many male workers either brought their wives and family with them or arranged for the sending of "picture brides."

The massive immigration of Japanese to the American mainland as well as Hawaii, then an independent monarchy, came much later. There were small numbers of Japanese in the United States in the 1860s and 1870s, but it took the 1885 decision of the Japanese government to allow Japanese to emigrate that brought about the explosive departure of tens of thousands of Japanese. Many Japanese emigrants first embarked for Hawaii, where there were well-advertised jobs for agricultural workers, before deciding to continue their journey to California where many found a permanent home.[2]

Prior to the 1885 legalization of Japanese emigration, the first attempt to move a mass of Japanese out of the country came in 1868 when several American labor contractors such as Hawaiian consul Robert W. Irwin together with diplomats such as Eugene Van Reed, who were working on behalf of sugar plantation owners in Hawaii, came to Japan looking for field workers. Van Reed illegally recruited 150 Japanese people (all but seven were young men) from the streets of Yokohama. Van Reed was able to sneak them out of the country and send them to work in Hawaii. Very few of the Japanese, however, were farmers, and most proved unsuited for plantation farming work. When the overseers began mistreating them, they protested, left the fields, and retreated to Honolulu. When the Japanese government heard of their poor treatment, it urged them to come home, even sending a large ship to pick them up. Ironically, most of the Hawaii-based Japanese chose to stay and gradually melted into the Hawaiian population.[3]

It was not that long until ethnic Japanese outnumbered Chinese in the United States and Hawaiians in their native land. Although there were far more ethnic Chinese in the United States throughout much of the nineteenth century, by 1910 there were 72,157 Japanese and 71,531 Chinese. The position of Japanese in Hawaii was even stronger by 1900, when they comprised 40 percent (61,111) of the entire population of the islands, outnumbering not only Chinese (25,767) but also native Hawaiians (29,799).[4]

Before the explosive growth of Japanese immigration to the United States that started in the 1880s and 1890s, only a small trickle of Japanese made their way to North America. We don't have access to exact figures, but American sources record the entry of only 335 Japanese through 1880, while Japanese authorities issued no more than 995 passports for travel to the United States during the 1860s and 1870s. It is possible that many Japanese with passports decided not to make the trip. These figures do not include short-term visits by such groups as an embassy of seventy-seven Japanese officials sent by the Meiji government to investigate life in North America and Europe in the early 1870s.[5]

Japanese who came for longer periods included a fair number of students who came to study in American high schools and colleges. Five young girls chosen by the new Meiji government accompanied the Japanese Iwakura Mission to the United States in 1871 to learn as much as they could about the United States and the West. Three of the girls stayed on for many years, and two of them studied at Vassar College.[6] A number of young Japanese men found a welcome haven at Rutgers University in New Jersey in the late 1860s. While there they encountered two American students at Rutgers, E. Warren Clark (1849–1907) and William Griffis (1843–1928) who after their graduation journeyed to Japan to become science teachers early in the 1870s and later become among the first Japanologists in the West.[7]

The earliest Japanese who found their way to the United States were fishermen and castaway sailors whose boats had been driven out to sea by the fierce storms that ravage the Japanese coastline. It was not uncommon for Japanese fishermen and sailors to get lost at sea, where most of them perished. Starting as early as 1830 a small number of these Japanese were picked up by American ships traveling to Hawaii and China. Two young Japanese men whose lives have been studied in great detail, Joseph Heco and Nakahama Manjiro, spent many years in the United States in the 1840s and 1850s after being rescued at sea by American ships. Heco in particular was educated in American schools and actually became an American citizen before later returning to Japan.[8]

THE GREAT DISCREPANCY IN HOW AMERICANS TREATED EARLY IMMIGRANTS AND LATER ARRIVALS

When a young Japanese man from Hawaii made a visit to California in the 1920s, he was shocked by the viciousness and anti-Japanese hostility he met the minute he got off the boat in San Francisco. He encountered intense racial verbal abuse wherever he went. There were pervasive cries of "Goddamn Jap," "Yellow Jap," "Dirty Jap." At railroad stations and in toilets he encountered ugly graffiti which included such expressions as "Japs Go Away" or "Fire the Japs." There were scribblings on sidewalks stating, "Japs, we don't want you" and a sign on a highway warned, "No more Japs wanted here."[9]

The attacks went far beyond mere words. One Japanese reported that "people even spit on Japanese in the streets. . . . In fact, I myself, was spit upon more than a few times." Another Issei exclaimed, "There was so much anti-Japanese feeling in those days! They called us 'Japs' and threw things at us. When I made a trip to Marysville [in California] to look for land, someone threw rocks." When Japanese went to rent or buy houses, they were turned away by realtors who told them, "If Japanese live around here, then the price of land will go down." Japanese often found themselves denied admittance at theaters and movie houses, and if they were able to get in, they could well be seated in special segregated sections with African Americans and other minorities. They often found themselves being pelted with stones or snowballs in cities, and their places of business often vandalized with their store windows smashed and the sidewalks out front smeared with horse manure.[10]

These harsh feelings did not reflect the far more positive response to the first Japanese who visited the United States in the 1860s and 1870s. It is evident that at least some Americans had a much more positive view of Japanese than they did of the Chinese in the 1860s and 1870s. This feeling began with the arrival of the Perry mission to Japan in 1853 and 1854. Commodore Perry and his crew were very impressed with their Japanese counterparts and felt that the Japanese were people with whom they could do business. Numerous Americans who went to Japan as teachers, missionaries, and the like took an almost instantaneous liking to the Japanese and sent back complimentary letters and articles and in time wrote books full of praise for the Japanese. They portrayed the Japanese as honest, hardworking, intelligent, and very quick to learn "Western ways."[11] William Elliot Griffis, hired as a science teacher in Japan and author of the first scholarly history of Japan in 1876, found the Japanese to be very intelligent, highly moral, most creative, highly organized, and well led. He deeply respected his students who were "surprisingly eager and earnest in school. They learn fast and study hard." Griffis's friend E. Warren Clark regarded Japanese as being very "Anglo-Saxon" in nature.[12]

Early Japanese immigrants to California were few in number and did not directly compete with white Americans or jobs. One can be quite astonished by the warm and highly complementary way that Americans received early Japanese visitors or early residents. The United States maintained good relations with Japan through the Russo-Japanese War (1904–1905), and Theodore Roosevelt unabashedly expressed support for the Japanese in that conflict.

These warm feelings toward the Japanese changed around the start of the last century when there was an explosion of Japanese immigration to Hawaii and the American mainland. Between 1885 and 1924, 380,000 Japanese immigrated to Hawaii and the continental United States. Japanese immigrants were the second-largest group of Asian immigrants to come to the United States during the late nineteenth and early twentieth centuries. Like Chinese and other Asian immigrants to the United States, most of the early Japanese immigrants were young, generally male *dekasegi* (sojourners) who had every intention of one day returning to their homeland once they had made their fortunes. Over time, however, they often settled down, called for their families to join them, and built strong ethnic communities such as "Japan Towns" (*Nihonmachi*) in San Francisco, Los Angeles, Sacramento, and Seattle. They tried to connect to both cultures by becoming more American while maintaining strong connections with their communities in Japan.[13]

Very much unlike the majority of American-born or European-born immigrants who arrived in California in family groups and came there to stay, the majority of early Japanese immigrants in the 1890s and early 1900s were younger single males, a status that allowed them to accept work as migratory workers such as lumberjacks, seasonal field hands, farmers and farm laborers, fishermen, and laborers for the railroads. They worked hard, lived in makeshift huts and bunkhouses, and took lower wages and still managed to save money to eventually open a small business, buy some land to farm on their own, or in some cases return to Japan.

Because Japan offered few opportunities for poor people to achieve financial success or social mobility, many first-generation Japanese came to North America with the hope of eventually becoming wealthy enough to return to Japan to buy a piece of land, to build their own house, and to live comfortably. It was hard work, and only a few managed to save enough money to return to Japan with their dreams fulfilled or to buy land and start farming on their own in California or elsewhere in the West. Those who decided to establish permanent roots in the United States often sought wives so that they could start families. One common way of accomplishing this was to recruit "picture brides" (*shashin-kekkon*) from Japan. This could be accomplished through an exchange of pictures and correspondence that might lead to a marriage by proxy and the wife traveling alone to North America to meet her husband for the first time in marriage.

Japanese worked a variety of jobs, including domestic service in big cities and as farmers. It is in agriculture in California that they really made their mark. Their most successful endeavors were in truck farming. In 1900, there were thirty-seven Japanese farms in the United States, mainly in California, with a combined acreage of only 4,674 acres. By 1910, however, Japanese owned 1,816 farms with a total acreage of 99,254. On the eve of World War II, they grew 95 percent of California's fresh snap beans and peas, 67 percent of the state's fresh tomatoes, and 44 percent of its onions. The most successful farmer was Kinji Ushijima, who gained the nickname the "Potato King." He arrived in California in 1887 with no money, but plenty of ambition. Working as a potato picker in the San Joaquin Valley, he eventually saved up enough money to buy a small plot of land that eventually grew into a major farm operation. By 1912 his farm had become huge. When he died in 1926, his estate was valued at $15 million.[14]

Unfortunately, the flood of Japanese entering California and other western states in the early 1900s brought a strong racist anti-Japanese response from many white residents. As long as the Japanese population remained small and worked as migrant farm workers, they were tolerated by the greater community. As they moved to sharecropping, to leasing the land, and to farm ownership, they became targets of sustained and organized anti-Japanese actions. Competition for jobs, inherent white racism, and other factors played into this problem. Japanese-American efforts to be fully accepted as Americans were generally unsuccessful. Japanese, like Chinese before them, quickly became the subjects of discriminatory laws at both state and federal levels that tried to restrict Japanese immigration and prohibiting them from becoming American citizens. They were denied membership in labor unions, and several western states went to great lengths to prohibit them from buying or leasing land.[15]

Historian Erika Lee writes:

> Japanese immigrants largely lost their struggle for equality in the United States, because no matter how hard they tried to demonstrate how American they were, they were still seen as Japanese. And with Japan growing as a world power that might actually threaten U.S. interests in the Pacific, Americans' views of Japan were increasingly negative. In this context, the threat of Japan and the threat of Japanese immigrants were linked together as part of a global discourse that would reshape immigration patterns, policies, and inter-national relations. What would become known as the "yellow peril" began in Germany.[16]

German Kaiser Wilhelm II coined the term "yellow peril" in 1895 following the conclusion of the Japanese victory over China in the Sino-Japanese War of 1894–1895. The Kaiser sent out urgent warnings of Japan's advances in the Pacific and warned of a flood of Japanese, Chinese, and other Asian immigrants who would in time completely overwhelm white people in North America and Europe.

Kaiser Wilhelm's message found a ready audience in the United States, especially in such western areas as California. Erika Lee writes:

> Apprehension about Japan's expanding empire heightened existing fears that Japanese immigrants were growing in number, taking away jobs, and preparing for an eventual invasion of the Western Hemisphere. These "yellow peril" anxieties became part of larger transnational conversations about hemispheric security and the future of the "white race" circulating throughout North and South America.[17]

The start of the twentieth century saw large-scale demonstrations and occasional violent riots against Japanese communities in the West. This discrimination against Japanese, including measures prohibiting them owning land or attending schools in the West, infuriated the Japanese government and hurt relations between Japan and the United States. President Theodore Roosevelt and the Japanese government finally arrived at the 1907 "Gentleman's Agreement" that would largely prohibit further Japanese immigration to the United States.

This "Yellow Peril" mentality is clearly exhibited in this turn-of-the-century California Industrial *Commission Report*:

> Close upon the retreat of the Chinese coolie, however, came the Japanese, equally menacing to the laboring interests of the country. Almost unnoticed, and without exciting either suspicion or alarm, has Japanese coolie labor crept into the country.... Every vessel from the Orient that touched at our western ports left large numbers of these little brown toilers upon our shores. They were sent out in gangs to the farming and fruit-growing districts, and almost before the white labor was aware that this new foe was among them, it found itself displaced by a new rival more dangerous than the Chinese.... [The Japanese] are more servile than the Chinese, but less obedient and far less desirable. They have most of the vices, with none of their virtues. They underbid the Chinese in everything, and are as a class tricky, unreliable and dishonest.[18]

Such feelings are a complete turnaround from the genuine warmth that greeted the early Japanese pioneers at Wakamatsu three decades earlier. But before large-scale Japanese immigration became a problem in the United States, relations between the United States and Japan were generally very good. Japan and Japanese received very good reviews in the American press as is indicated in the press coverage of the Wakamatsu colonists in 1869–1871. The Japanese who arrived in San Francisco in May 1869 and then moved to Gold Hill to the Wakamatsu colony received a cordial, even warm, welcome from the white Americans they met. Several contemporary newspaper reports convey in glowing terms how the press viewed these early newcomers to California.

THE WAKAMATSU JAPANESE ARE WARMLY WELCOMED

California newspapers, especially the San Francisco–based *Daily Alta California*, played an important role in introducing the newly arrived Japanese to the people of northern California. Since other newspapers elsewhere in the United States and Canada copied these stories, the arrival of Japanese soon became well known across North America. The positive reporting by these newspapers probably influenced many of their readers in their view of Japanese.

The *Daily Alta California* of May 27, 1869, reported that three Japanese families had arrived safely in San Francisco and that larger groups would be coming at a later date. Described as a free people "who have never been serfs," these Japanese were characterized in a positive light:

> This whole Japanese party is dignity incarnate. By their nature they are a people who will put up with no insult or deception; that must always be borne in mind. It is dangerous to treat Japanese in the same fashion as Chinese. With their industry and highly developed skills, they have come with their families to help develop our resources.[19]

Other newspapers in the region published similarly laudatory accounts of the new immigrants. They also lavished attention and praise on John Henry Schnell's Japanese wife Jou. She had "refined delicacy, very pretty forms and features, and a very winning address." They added that she was also "healthy, frugal, industrious, and very affectionate." These newspaper reporters had only met her once before writing these stories and there was certainly a language barrier that made direct communication with Jou impossible, but they nevertheless endowed her with the "idealized domestic virtues of a married American woman."[20]

This early praise continued on into October 1869. The *Daily Alta California* of October 24, 1869, reported:

> The Japanese are intelligent as we are. They are brave, industrious, and economical. They have a sort of cooperative principal which maintains the dignity of labor and takes away much of its subservience. They will win universal respect by sort of a heathenish habit of minding their own business. . . . The neighbors like these people, and give them a hearty welcome. Every packet carrier to Japan brings earnest entreaties [by Americans] for their friends to come to a country where everybody is free to do as he likes. . . . [The Japanese in America] say [in letters to other Japanese in Japan] "You have heard of Heaven away oft. We have found that place. Come and share our happiness."

In June the same newspaper commented on the nature of Japanese society soon after the arrival of Schnell, his Japanese wife and daughter, and six other Japanese in San Francisco. The newspaper published a very favorable account of the Japanese colonists, calling them eminently qualified to become leading members of American society:[21]

> [An unidentified French correspondent writes to us.]
>
> "Unlike other Eastern peoples, there is something about the Japanese that is congenial to Europeans. Having spent some years in Japan, with opportunities of official position to observe the higher classes, we pronounce them in no way our inferiors. The men are dignified, well-educated, exceedingly polite, brave and full of ingenuity. The women have refined delicacy, very pretty forms and features, and a very winning address. They are scrupulously neat in their persons and in their housekeeping. Their accomplishments are quite up to our standard. They are healthy, frugal, industrious, and very affectionate. In any of the refined circles of the capitals of Europe, we know a hundred Japanese ladies that would command their own choice of husbands. Not only does one

admire their personal charms, but they would in the eye of matrimony be endorsed by the absence of the expensive habits that, in our own belles, interpose so terrible an obstacle to marriage."

Madame Schnell is a Japanese lady, evidently of that class that inspired the eloquent description we have quoted.

If the introduction of new branches of culture and industry, and the utilization of lands hitherto neglected as of little value, are beneficial to California, we may well welcome this first colony from Japan. They interfere with no existing occupations. They are not an inferior race. They are unlike other Asiatics in many important respects. They at once adopt our customs and they come with their families to make permanent homes and investment. Their earnings will be invested here and not abroad. There is nothing repellant about them, but much that is attractive and winning in their bearing and their manner of address. They have no bigotry, and if by Christian treatment we prove the excellence of our religion, they are just such a people as will be likely to take kindly to our religious instruction.

A writer for the San Francisco-based *Daily Morning Call* visited the Wakamatsu colony in early January 1870, about seven months into its operations. He came away with the following positive impressions:[22]

In my last [article] I mentioned the peculiarly neat habits of the Japanese in their household management, and this neatness strikes the beholder both indoors and out. In their persons they are scrupulously cleanly, and do not offend the sight or smell with the dirty, greasy blouses that render the Chinese so offensive. All of their out-buildings, work-shops, tools, and agricultural implements, are constructed with an eye to their neat appearance, and are kept in the best possible manner. A long row of chicken coops that an American would hastily construct of refuse lumber and old lathe, and ornament possibly with a coat of whitewash is with the Japanese rather an ornamental affair. The one I saw was constructed of narrow strips of pine, not over a half-inch wide, all smoothly planed and beaded on both edges, and put together with most extraordinary neatness; and still giving it a frail, "bird-cage" appearance, while the nests were as nicely pinned, neatly joined, and dovetailed as the Japanese toy boxes that ornament the shop windows on Montgomery Street [in San Francisco], showing an appreciation for the comfort of the fowl that occupy them, that it were the basest kind of ingratitude in said fowl not to repay by request "chanting of its lay."

The yards not only about the houses, but also around the stables and chicken-coops, are as smooth and as clean as an asphalt sidewalk. Every morning they are swept and not a chip or a twig of any stock of uncleanliness, or evidence of slovenly habits, is apparent, and a lady could promenade over the ground without experiencing half the danger of soiling her linen skirts that she would from the "old Sogers" and tobacco spittle of a fashionable American promenade. In their habits they are steadily industrious, and their family relations—I speak of those at Gold Hill—are as sacredly observed as among more "civilized" people. The men are all expert gardeners, the carpenters included, and I saw the Doctor of the Colony pruning grape vines with a remarkable skill, in which, Mr. Schnell informed me, he is equaled by them all.

This doctor[23]—the Li-Po-Tai of the Colony—is said to have achieved considerable success in healing cutaneous diseases, and uses only vegetable compounds which are guaranteed to do no harm, even if they do not work a cure, a fact the knowledge of which must be exceedingly comfort to the patient in these days of quacks and mineral poisons in the shape of patient nostrums. We spent some two hours in the company of Mr. Schnell, and were much edified by the information which he gave me. At present he is experiencing considerable trouble with the miners who for the sake of their "dollar" diggings," have ruthlessly invaded his plantation in many places and sadly interfered with his operations.

Writers for the Placerville *Mountain Democrat* notified their readers that "We can see no particular objection to the presence of any people in our midst who are willing to contribute the result of their learning, experience and skill in increasing the variety of our useful productions." These writers went as far as to congratulate the colonists for "adopt[ing] the habits and customs of the American people."[24]

These favorable impressions of the Japanese as a model community may also have been another way that newspaper editors could further deprecate the far more numerous Chinese. The editors of the Placerville *Mountain Democrat* proclaimed that the Japanese were "intelligent and industrious—of entirely a different character from the Chinese who came to this country." They had a desire to "assimilate . . . with American ideas and customs" while Chinese were supposedly "tenacious of their pagan rites and ideas." A San Francisco paper complained that Chinese "circumscribe the opportunities for employment to white men" and so praised the Japanese because they would not "enter into competition" with white labor with their plans for tea and silk production.[25]

NOTES

1. John E. Van Sant, *Pacific Pioneers: Japanese Journeys to America and Hawaii, 1850–80* (Urbana and Chicago: University of Illinois Press, 2000), 133.

2. One motivation for emigration out of Japan was the heavy burden of taxes imposed by the Meiji government on farmers. Farmers paid the price of Japan's modernization, but for many farmers the taxes were a real imposition they could not pay for and the alternative was bankruptcy and loss of their land. Immigration provided a convenient escape for this.

3. Paul Spickard, *Japanese Americans: The Formation and Transformations of an Ethnic Group* (New York: Twayne Publishers, 1996), 10.

4. Ronald Takaki, *Strangers from a Different Shore: A History of Asian America* (New York: Back Bay Books, 1998), 179–80.

5. Van Sant, *Pacific Pioneers*, 2–3.

6. For further details see Janice P. Nimura, *Daughters of the Samurai: A Journey from East to West and Back* (New York: W. W. Norton, 2015).

7. See E. Warren Clark, *Life and Adventure in Japan* (New York: American Tract Society, 1878).

8. For further details, see Van Sant, *Pacific Pioneers*, 3–4.

9. Takaki, *Strangers*, 179–80.

10. Takaki, *Strangers*, 181–82.

11. See, for example, Clark, *Life and Adventure in Japan*.

12. William Elliot Griffis, *The Mikado's Empire: History of Japan and Personal Experiences, Observations and Studies in Japan 1870–1874* (New York: Harper & Brothers, 1883), 501–2.

13. Erika Lee, *The Making of Asian America: A History* (New York: Simon & Schuster, 2015), 109.

14. Lee, *Making*, 119.

15. Lee, *Making*, 119–20.

16. Lee, *Making*, 123.

17. Lee, *Making*, 124. Later, when entry into the United States was closed, tens of thousands of Japanese migrated to South America, mainly Brazil. Today there are over 1.5 million ethnic Japanese in Brazil. See Hugo Cordova Quero et al., eds., *Transnational Faiths: Latin American Immigrants and Their Religions in Japan* (Farnham, UK: Ashgate, 2014).

18. Quoted in Kevin Wildie, *Sacramento's Historic Japantown: Legacy of a Lost Neighborhood* (Charleston, SC: The History Press, 2013), 26.

19. *Daily Alta California*, May 27, 1869.

20. Van Sant, *Pacific Pioneers*, 125.

21. *Daily Alta California*, June 16, 1869.

22. "Up in El Dorado," *Daily Morning Call*, January 3, 1870. No author listed.

23. Unfortunately I have not been able to establish the identity of this doctor. Perhaps he was Japanese? Li Po-Tai (1817–1893) was a Chinese-born doctor who practiced Chinese medicine in San Francisco from the Gold Rush era until his death. He had many patients and died a wealthy man. Source: *San Francisco Call*, March 20, 1893.

24. Quoted in Van Sant, *Pacific Pioneers*, 125–26.

25. Van Sant, *Pacific Pioneers*, 126.

Chapter Four

The Founding of the Wakamatsu Tea and Silk Colony Farm

The bitter 1868 defeat of Aizu left its people in desperate shape and John Henry Schnell with no further future in Japan. Schnell had fought for the losing side, and it is very possible that he was no longer welcome in Japan. Furthermore, since the cessation of the Boshin War had deprived him of his trade as an arms dealer, the time to leave Japan was now. Schnell was both a gambler and a risk taker, and it is not surprising that he would take immediate actions to resolve his plight. He had his family to take care of—his Japanese wife Jou and their baby daughter Frances. They had another baby, a daughter Mary, the first known child of a Japanese parent born in the United States, born in the spring of 1870.

Schnell also realized that there were a lot of bitter and desperate people in Aizu who had lost everything and had no place to go and nothing to do. It was at this time, late 1868 or early 1869, that Schnell probably came up with the idea of establishing a sizable colony of Aizu settlers in California who would produce tea and silk. These two products were in hot demand in the United States, and he possibly thought that a Japanese enterprise there producing those goods might have a good chance of success. The people of Aizu had lost so much after their bitter defeat, so a successful venture in a new and faraway land could provide them with a chance to start a new life. Some claim that the former Daimyo Matsudaira liked and endorsed the idea and that he may have provided Schnell with some seed money to help pay for supplies to take to America and for the passage of the Japanese workers working on the farm, but there is no proof of this claim. It is evident that the new Meiji government confiscated Matsudaira's remaining wealth and land after the defeat and put him under house arrest. The defeated Matsudaira certainly had no money and was in no position to fund the California experiment, though it is possible that the *daimyo* supplied Schnell with funding before his defeat and capture.[1]

Today we know little or nothing about Schnell's status in Japan after November 1868: Was he a wanted man? Was he forced to leave the country? Did the new Meiji government know or even care about his plans for a Japanese colony in California? We will probably never have any definite answers to these questions. But we do know that Schnell traveled from Aizu to Yokohama with his wife Jou and their daughter Frances sometime in late 1868 or early 1869, possibly going by ship from the Japan Sea port of Niigata to Yokohama around northern Honshu. While in Yokohama he bought supplies for the farm in California and secured passage for himself, his family, and six other Japanese on the PMSS *China*.[2] They left Yokohama in late April and arrived in San Francisco three weeks later.

The arrival of John Henry Schnell, his Japanese wife Jou, their daughter Frances, and six other Japanese attracted considerable attention in the newspapers of northern California. San Francisco and northern California were teeming with tens of thousands of Chinese but only an occasional Japanese. The *Daily Alta California* newspaper published an article about the newly arrived Japanese on May 27, 1869, just a week after their arrival. A lengthy page one article proclaimed:

> Arrival of Japanese Immigrants
>
> Three Japanese Families—Thirty More Coming Soon—Probability That The Defeated Prince Will Follow—Japan No Home For Them Since The Civil War
>
> A Prussian gentleman, Herr Schnell by name, who for ten years lived in the northern part of Japan, has landed in San Francisco with three Japanese families. These three families form the advance guard of a group of forty families now on its way to this port. Eighty more families are to follow, making a total of 120 families and four hundred persons coming to California to establish a permanent colony here.
>
> Most of them are silk producers, while some are cultivators of tea. They have brought with them 50,000 three-year-old *kuwa* trees, which . . . are used in the production of high quality silk. . . . Besides these, 500 three-year old, five-feet saplings of the wax tree and six million tea seeds are coming later. These Japanese, far from being serfs, are free people. Should the prince of Aizu come, many more immigrants and their families are due to follow.[3]

The article gives Schnell's position as "Interpreting Secretary to the Prussian Legation and Laterally Minister of Finance to the Northern Principalities at war with the Mikado." The paper reports that "Herr Schnell means to buy Government land, not in the valleys, which are unsuited, but in the cheaper hill or mountain lands," but there is no mention of Schnell's position as an arms dealer in Japan.[4]

More than her husband, Jou Schnell, then twenty-three or twenty-four, caught the attention of the press. She was one of the first Japanese women to venture to the United States. She was married to a handsome German and had a baby girl. There was no talking to her through the language barrier, but the press endowed her with a vast array of virtues.[5] They lavished attention and praise on John Henry Schnell's Japanese wife Jou. She had "refined delicacy, very pretty forms and features, and a very winning address." They added that she was also "healthy, frugal, industrious, and very affectionate." These newspaper reporters had only met her once before writing these stories, and there was certainly a language barrier that made direct communication with Jou impossible, but they nevertheless endowed her with the "idealized domestic virtues of a married American woman."[6] Sadly, after an initial burst of attention in the press, she disappeared into history without any trace of what kind of person she was. The last we hear about her is in the spring of 1870 when she gave birth to her second daughter, Mary, the first child born in North America with a Japanese parent.

The news of Schnell's arrival with some Japanese and promises of dozens more on their way attracted the attention of newspapers in Sacramento and elsewhere which expressed an interest in having the Japanese build their colony in their neck of the woods. A correspondent for the *Sacramento Daily Union* writing from Placerville extolled the virtues of El Dorado County with an unabashed boosterism:

> In El Dorado we have thousands of acres of as fine and productive land as can be wished for, capable of producing grapes, apples, pears, plums, and all the smaller kinds of fruits and vegetables in perfection, and corn, wheat, barley, and other cereals are grown to great advantage. Can there be any better climate for silk culture or the growing of the tea plant than in this and adjoining counties? Our delightful, clear, warm days and comfortable nights, from April to November, with all the luxuries that a rich and productive soil, if properly tilled, will give, must and will soon be sought after by those who want homes. It is to be hoped that . . . Mr. Schnell and his Japanese associates will give our county a visit before settling elsewhere.[7]

As predicted in these accounts, additional Japanese workers arrived in late October 1869 and made their way to Wakamatsu Farm. According to one report in the *Daily Alta California*, dated October 24, 1869, thirteen men, women, and children, newly arrived from Japan, had to wait in San Francisco until Schnell could come to pick them up.[8] The local newspaper, the *Mountain Democrat,* announced that on October 30, 1869, sixteen Japanese arrived at the tea colony. It is hard to determine which count is more accurate, but based on the census taken two months later, the sixteen figure seems more likely.

The courtship of this promising new enterprise did not last long. The following news story in the *Daily Alta California* for June 8, 1869, announced Schnell's purchase of the Graner farm in Gold Hill:

> Messrs. Schnell and Bennett, agent and managers for the Japanese families, now en route for this State, have purchased the ranch of Charles Grainor, near Gold Hill, in this county, paying five thousand dollars therefor. They express themselves highly pleased with the location for all the purposes contemplated—silk and tea culture. They design increasing their area to at least two thousand acres. The nature of the ground in that locality will admit of this, thus giving them nearly or quite a connected plantation of that diameter.

WHAT THE COLONISTS SAW ON THEIR WAY TO GOLD HILL

When Schnell, his family, and the first groups of Japanese colonists arrived at their farm site near Coloma, they found a region in transition. Several thousand gold miners had come and gone since the advent of the gold rush in 1848–1849, and area residents were busy making the transition from mining to agriculture. A writer for the *Daily Morning Call* described the landscape on his way to the Wakamatsu Farm Colony, journeying by the Sacramento Valley Railroad to Shingle Springs (about ten miles from Coloma) and then by stage to Coloma:[9]

> (January 1, 1870) Our road lay through a region torn and washed away by mining operations, presenting an appearance of desolation, as desolate as can well be imagined. On every hand was the dry, red-brick-dust soil, the heaps of cobbles, trickling of muddy waters, and remnants of homes, sluices and mining cabins—all pointing to what had been and the absence of population signifying what is.
>
> We passed by abandoned claims without number, deserted cabins crumbling in pieces, and even through towns which gave no signs of human occupancy. Cold Spring,[10] about two miles from Placerville, was formerly a flourishing mining camp and polled eight hundred votes. Now one would suppose it to be entirely deserted, but for the appearance of half a dozen Chinamen milling a few rods off. Gold Hill was also a lively camp, with brick buildings and other substantial evidences of prosperity. Now the town proper does not seem to number a score of inhabitants. The miners . . . here say that this was once a district noted for its mineral wealth, and has been the scene of countless rich strikes. Now they are making perhaps $2 a day, barely enough to keep them in grub. Agriculture and viniculture have taken a share in this section of the county, and mining is fast taking a back seat before their rapid strides. It is here that the Japanese colony has commenced operations and introduced the culture of tea upon California soil. . . .
>
> (January 2, 1870) When I closed my letter yesterday, we had arrived at Gold Hill, El Dorado County, formerly one of the richest mining regions of the

State, now comparatively deserted, and its mines mostly abandoned. But Gold Hill bids fair to enter upon a new era of prosperity, not with the rush that first characterized her coming into public prominence, but by the slow and sure process that agriculture insures when the proper opportunities are offered. Gold Hill appears to be a valley to one coming from the high mountains in that region, because of its low situation topographically; but the country is rolling and gives evidence of the foundation for great agricultural wealth. Where the land is not torn up and stripped of its surface by miners, vines and fruit trees are planted, gardens are cultivated, and the scene resembles those peculiar localities known as "cow counties." But cow counties are not to be despised, and the day has gone by when the proud and aristocratic mining counties could look down upon them with contempt.

Agriculture has grown to be a giant, while mining has wasted its best energies, and stands old and decrepit in the presence of its youthful and vigorous competitor. None appreciate this wonderful change more than the miners, and they are filled with sadness that the days of lucky strikes and big nuggets are nearly at an end. They feel it also in their pockets—those whose pockets are not empty, and hence devoid of sensitiveness—and many of them are trying to struggle out of the current in which they have been so long drifting to no purpose, and fall into the agricultural tide, which they believe to be their tide in the affairs of man, which if taken at the flood, leads on to fortune. With this object in view they have settled upon large tracts of land, and in their spare hours, when the elements and other causes prevent mining operations, they devote themselves to clearing off their land, planting vines, and at least preparing a home and a place to lay their heads. Many vineyards, and orchards, and gardens are growing up in this vicinity, which promise to be attractive not only on account of their homelike qualities to their owners, but exceedingly profitable as well.

BUYING LAND AND SETTLING DOWN

Because of the lack of official records, it is unclear exactly who arrived at the Wakamatsu farm near Coloma and when they arrived. We know that there were six Japanese and Schnell and his family during the summer of 1869. Some, if not all, of their supplies arrived later that summer on the same or another ship from Japan. Unfortunately for the enterprise, the former Aizu daimyo Matsudaira did not to come to California after he received a pardon from the new Meiji government in 1869. Without his patronage and his presence in California, the Wakamatsu colony probably lost an opportunity to attract the large numbers of settlers anticipated by Schnell and the California newspaper editors.

It is known that sixteen more settlers from Aizu arrived in the autumn of 1869 and that a smaller third group (probably numbering less than ten) arrived during the latter part of summer or fall of 1870. According to the 1870 census taken in Coloma on July 1, there were twenty-two Japanese living with Schnell and his family in the Gold Hill District of Coloma.[11] This report likely refers to the original party who came with Schnell plus the second group of sixteen who came in the autumn of 1869.

When the initial party of Schnell, his family, and several Japanese arrived in San Francisco, they wasted no time in trying to find a home for their enterprise. Somehow Schnell heard that former Coloma-area farmer Charles Graner was selling his land and farm in Gold Hill. According to the deed of sale signed on June 18, 1869, by Charles M. Graner and J. Henry Schnell, Schnell made a down payment of $500 with a promise to pay the full sum of $5,000 (about $85,000 in 2018 dollars) at some future date. Through this agreement Schnell bought 160 acres of land from Graner.[12]

The *Daily Alta California* of June 16, 1869, announced the purchase of the Graner house and property for $5,000 and mentioned several of the features of the purchase:

* 600 acres under fence[13]
* A large orchard of seven-year-old trees
* 50,000 bearing vines not needing irrigation
* Plenty of grain fields and abundant water
* A good brick house well-furnished and a barn
* Implements of husbandry and horses, cows, pigs and fowls

The article reports that Mr. Schnell intended to build a house for every family with its own garden and its own silkworms which the families would deliver to a common factory for processing. Additionally, Schnell planned to open a nursery for the sale of Japanese plants. The article also reports, "The very first day these people laid out a lake for fish culture on their new purchase, there being a well-adapted spot among the undulations of the land. The lake was to be held together with a cement of shell-lime, sand and ashes. Additionally, the Japanese varnish tree and hill rice will be introduced."[14]

JAPANESE LIVING AT THE WAKAMATSU FARM IN JULY 1870

As a result of the 1870 national census, we are fortunate today to have a complete list of Japanese living at the Wakamatsu Colony Farm as of early July 1870. We cannot be sure of their names because the census taker clearly did not know how to pronounce Japanese, and the Japanese, obviously not literate in English, could not correct what Schnell told him. The handwriting of the census taker is also rather poor, which makes transcribing the names all the more difficult. These facts make it very hard to trace the origins and ultimate fate of these Japanese workers.

Nevertheless, we can learn something about them. Excluding the very young children, the Japanese residents ranged in age from eighteen to forty-nine with a median age of about twenty-nine or thirty. There were four married couples and four young children, all girls. Almost all of them are listed as farm laborers except for two who are listed as carpenters.

Another group of Japanese, probably numbering no more than ten, arrived at the Wakamatsu farm sometime during the summer or early autumn of 1870—certainly after the census was taken. We do not have their names,

Table 4.1. Names of Japanese Living at the Wakamatsu Tea and Silk Colony Farm in July 1870

Name	Age	Sex	Occupation
Jou Schnell	24	F	
Frances	2	F	
Mary	2 months	F	
Nishijara Taro	18	M	Laborer
Kingdelryo	29	M	Carpenter
Mrs. Kingdelryo	24	F	
Daidjiro	46	M	Carpenter
Mrs. Daidjiro	42	F	
Takidado (daughter of Mr. and Mrs. Daidjiro)	2	F	
Tomodgaro	29	M	Farm Laborer
Sinsia	43	M	Farm Laborer
Mrs. Sinsia	49	F	Farm Laborer
Sindryo	23	M	Farm Laborer
Mrs. Sindryo	20	F	Farm Laborer
Tasnezero	32	M	Farm Laborer
Kintaro	25	M	Farm Laborer
Junyaro	19	M	Farm Laborer
Flyzero	23	M	Farm Laborer
Wozezoro	31	M	Farm Laborer
Amanin (possibly wife of Wozezoro)	30	F	Farm Laborer
Child (possibly daughter of Wozezoro-Amarisa)	7	F	
Masemuzu (probably Masumizu)	26	M	Farm Laborer
Amesabra	23	M	Farm Laborer
Pakeyee	23	M	Farm Laborer

Source: U.S. Census for 1870 for Coloma, Eldorado County, California. Listed online at Ancestry.com (accessed May 1, 2017).

but it's possible one of them was Okei Ito, who came to be a nurse for Jou Schnell's two baby girls.

SOCIAL ORIGINS OF THE JAPANESE

Although scholars today have a great deal of information about the general aspects of the Wakamatsu Tea and Silk Farm Colony, we know surprisingly little about the social origins and lives of the Japanese workers who accompanied Schnell and his family to Gold Hill. The names on the census list (table 4.1) give us some idea of their ages and responsibilities while at the Colony Farm. But as far as we know, they did not leave any written records about themselves. The best we can rely on are the many newspaper accounts by reporters curious about these folks from an alien land.

There are wildly different stories about these Japanese. It is said that Schnell's wife Jou was the daughter of a samurai or other high-ranking Aizu domain official. That is very likely since the Daimyo Matsudaira gave Schnell the honorary status of a samurai due to his service in selling arms to Aizu and training Aizu samurai in their use. The fact that Jou acquired a nursemaid (Okei Ito) to help with her daughters is a further sign of her higher social status both in Japan and California.

But what about the others? Legends persist that at least some of the Japanese at the Wakamatsu farm were samurai, but that is highly unlikely. The conception and implementation of the Tea and Silk Farm was the full responsibility of Schnell and only Schnell. He was taking a calculated risk by taking a group of workers to California and starting a commercial enterprise, but he clearly did not have enough money to make it work. He knew there was a high demand for Japanese tea and silk in the United States, and he had probably heard that the state government of California was paying bounties to farmers who planted mulberry trees. He possibly hoped that the bounties might give him enough capital to carry through with his project.

It makes sense that Schnell would only hire people with farming, tea-growing, and silk-producing experience.[15] It would have been irrational for him to bring over samurai who had little or no experience in farming or tea and silk production although it was not unheard of for some samurai to have training in such fields as farming and carpentry. It is entirely possible that one or more of the colonists was a samurai because a samurai sword was left at the farm when the workers left. Nevertheless, the census list corroborates the supposition that most of the workers were commoners by identifying the professions of the people as carpenters and farm laborers. As ordinary citizens of Aizu Domain, they had lost everything when the imperial army destroyed their city as well as neighboring farms and villages. Schnell offered to take them safely away to another land where they might get a fresh start.

The farmers and carpenters—several sources state that there were four carpenters and that the rest were farm workers—had firm contracts, jobs, and good prospects at getting food and shelter. But unfortunately their expectations were not met. Their small monthly wages of about four dollars was hardly adequate for life in California, so that by June 1871 virtually all but two of them had moved away from the colony.[16] Sadly, we have very little information about most of their lives after they left the Wakamatsu farm.

HOUSING THE COLONISTS

When the erstwhile reporter from the San Francisco–based *Daily Morning Call* visited the Wakamatsu Farm Colony in early January 1870, he took special note of their housing plans. Although the farm house was quite spacious, there was by no means enough room for all the settlers. According to this article, the colony's four carpenters were hard at work building what was to be housing for the workers:

> Up to this time, the Japanese have accommodated themselves in their household manners at considerable inconvenience, but this will soon be at an end, and in a few weeks they will be settled down as comfortably as you please, with houses of their own, each family reposing 'under its own vine and fig tree.' Among their number are four carpenters, and these men are now engaged in erecting buildings for the use of the party. The houses are to be twelve in number, dimensions 36 feet by 30, each containing four rooms, and built in the Japanese fashion with low, pitched roofs, the eves extending far over the sills, and forming a balcony, or awning, around the entire house. . . . The partition walls are of paper, the outer walls of wood; one room is to be used as a sleeping room, another as a kitchen, and the two others—in each house—for silk raising, where the worms will be kept and nursed and the silk reeled and otherwise manipulated.
>
> The Japanese carpenters are ingenious workmen, and their work is done with marvelous neatness. A curious feature of their houses is that they do not contain a nail, all the joints and timbers being dovetailed together by many ingenious devices, and the whole work, even to the rafters, is as smooth as if polished down with sand paper. And the Japanese are neat people, for they use no paint to hide any blemishes of construction or ornamentation. . . . Every morning, as regularly as she cooks breakfast, or sweeps the floor, the Japanese housewife takes a wet cloth and scours the interior of the entire dwelling, leaving no part untouched, and no stain or dirty spot to mar its cleanly appearance. The Japanese do not come into the houses with muddy boots, after the style of the American 'sovereign,' but having covered the floor with a neat matting, always remove the dirty sandals before stepping upon it. . . .
>
> They are bright, intelligent and polite, lifting their hats and bowing gracefully to strangers, and the women stay at home, do the cooking, take care of

the babies, keep the house in order, and manage pretty much as American housewives do.... Take them all in all, they are in every respect a superior race to the Chinese, and resemble them in no manner except their physical appearance.[17]

As the writer notes, there was a crash effort to build housing for the workers because there was no room for them all in the farm house. There is some reference to the fact that upon arrival, many of the workers had to camp outside for quite some time, perhaps in tents, but after being there for a few months they could now look forward to some basic housing.

THE MYSTERY CONTINUES

The real tragedy here is that we know so little about the Japanese colonists. We only know a few of their names, but next to nothing about their occupations, and their thoughts and feelings. The result is that this or any similar historical or sociological study must remain hollow at its core. The only person to whom we can relate even slightly is John Henry Schnell because journalists interviewed him at length, but even he went bankrupt and disappeared without a trace. He left no written record and even abandoned the one person—Okei Ito—he had brought over to care for his baby daughters.

Fortunately for us, the Japanese visited a photography studio in Placerville during their stay where several of them posed for pictures. We can look into their eyes and imagine who or what they were, but the pictures come without names. There is even a picture of a young woman aged perhaps eighteen to twenty. The lack of any information about most of the Japanese creates a situation where several modern writers have written fictional accounts of life at the Wakamatsu Colony. The most notable of these stories are Joan Barton Barsotti's children's book, *Okei-San: A Girl's Journey, Japan to California, 1868–1870*; Herb Tanimoto's *Keiko's Kimono: A Doll's Journey to America in 1869 with the Wakamatsu Tea and Silk Colony*; and Yoshiko Uchida's *Samurai of Gold Hill*.

A more contemporaneous and less speculative depiction of the Japanese colonists comes from the imagination of the many American journalists who wrote about the farm colony. The idea of a Japanese colony suddenly appearing in California caught the attention of these writers—it was too good a story to ignore. Collectively, they created a very favorable image of the Japanese. They were educated and honorable people, honest and hardworking, who came from a noble land. They were anxious to learn about their new country and quickly adapted themselves to American culture. They were no threat to American workers because there were no other practicing tea and silk farms anywhere in California. They had highly refined tastes and practiced good manners and clearly came from a highly cultured civilization.

They got on well with their neighbors, lived in immaculate homes, and were welcoming and friendly to American visitors.

To some degree these assessments of the Japanese settlers reflect broad cultural attitudes. The Wakamatsu colony came at a time where Japanese art and culture were greatly admired throughout Western Europe and North America. Japonism or Japonisme is a French term that was first used by Jules Claretie in his book *L'Art Francais en 1872*. It refers to the influence of Japanese art on Western art and culture and describes the craze for all things Japanese that permeated the West during most of the latter part of the Victorian period. Many people in the West had a glamorous image of Japan which lacked much basis in reality. Oscar Wilde's comment "The whole of Japan is a pure invention. There is no such country, there are no such people" made note of the false image that so many people had of Japan.

This image of the Japanese probably influenced the way in which these American journalists saw the Wakamatsu colonists. They knew nothing about the Japanese, but because of that culture's positive reputation, felt inclined to share these very positive qualities and perpetuate these general stereotypes. Many other newspapers across the United States reprinted these stories, which meant that for a very brief period the Wakamatsu Colony became known across America.

Besides benefiting from these broad, supportive political and cultural attitudes toward the Japanese, the initial reputation of the Wakamatsu Colony and the curious respect for its residents might also reflect some of nineteenth-century America's widespread curiosity and general enthusiasm for experimental "utopian" communities—Brook Farm, Oneida, New Harmony, Amana, and Helicon Home Colony are among the best known. As early as 1878, sociologist William A. Hinds catalogued forty-six distinct intentional communities in his study *American Communities and Co-operative Colonies*, a groundbreaking work which he expanded and revised in 1902 and again in 1908. Almost without exception, these niche communities were established in rural settings, in an effort to reimagine and reinvigorate such American ideals as democracy, free enterprise, and freedom of religion apart from the growing challenges of industrial urbanization. While most of these intentional communities were founded on a particular religious or socially progressive agenda shared by their members, in other significant ways the Wakamatsu Colony fit the general outlines of this phenomenon. It enjoyed a charismatic, compelling leader in the figure of John Henry Schnell. Its colonists were bound together by a common cultural identity. Its identity as a niche community included both a residential society with a shared economic enterprise. It appears to have been regarded, at least initially, as having the potential to produce a model community that would cooperate in a productive way with the greater society surrounding it. However, as has already been established, unlike the majority of these other nineteenth-century intentional communities, the Wakamatsu Colony was not a worker-owned cooperative.

It seems curious, therefore, that most contemporary journalists would mistakenly characterize it as such. Did they make that assumption based on their understanding of these other cooperative communities? Did John Henry Schnell actively propagate that notion? At the very least, he does not appear to have been very aggressive in correcting that false assumption. Viewed against the backdrop of these other American experiments in communal living, John Henry Schnell's transportation of displaced Japanese workers in support of his own entrepreneurial enterprise might easily gain additional curiosity and respect from the assumption that Wakamatsu was a worker-owned cooperative. This would create a situation where it becomes a noble and modern social and economic experiment that falls squarely within the nineteenth-century American vogue of intentional and cooperative societies.

NOTES

1. John E. Van Sant, *Pacific Pioneers: Japanese Journeys to America and Hawaii, 1850–80* (Urbana and Chicago: University of Illinois Press, 2000), 122.
2. The PMSS *China* made regular runs between Hong Kong, Yokohama, and San Francisco. It often carried over eight hundred passengers, a third in first class and most of the rest—mainly Chinese—in steerage.
3. *Daily Alta California News*, May 27, 1869.
4. *Daily Alta California*, May 27, 1869.
5. Quoted in Van Sant, *Pacific Pioneers*, 125.
6. Van Sant, *Pacific Pioneers*, 125.
7. "Letter from Placerville" in the *Sacramento Daily Union*, June 5, 1869.
8. I have heard rumors that Schnell may have made a quick trip to Japan a few months after his arrival, but there is no hard evidence of that. Perhaps if he went, it was to retrieve these additional Japanese workers.
9. "Up in El Dorado," *Daily Morning Call*, January 1–2, 1870.
10. Cold Springs (formerly Cold Spring) is a census-designated place in El Dorado County, California, located four miles west of Placerville. It had a 1910 population of 446. A post office operated at Cold Spring from 1852 to 1874.
11. See the actual sheet for the 1870 U.S. census listed on Amazon.com. Gold Hill is located between two to three miles from Coloma. It was one of the small towns that sprang up with the 1848–1849 gold rush. The town had a very brief existence. It attracted a large number of gold miners between 1849 and the mid-1850s, but their numbers shrank rapidly when the miners could find no more gold and moved on to more promising sites. Prospectors built an irrigation canal in the town to bring water to the region to help with mining. A later benefit of the canal is that it played a key role in helping the area become good for fruit growing. The land became a rich farm area after the prospectors left. The only evidence today of the town of Gold Hill is the remains of a single stone building and a few residences. Source: Nancy Dunk (compiler), *At the Heart of Gold Country: Placerville and Its Surrounding Area* (Placerville: El Dorado County Historical Society, 2013).
12. See the appendix for a copy of the deed and for a more detailed discussion of land transactions. Scholar John Van Sant and a few others claim that Schnell bought 640 acres of land, but the consensus is that Schnell purchased 160 acres. See Van Sant, *Pacific Pioneers*, 125.
13. In fact Schnell bought 160 acres from Mr. Graner.

14. "The Japanese Settlement," *Daily Alta California*, June 16, 1869. The newspaper also reports that a highly competent native doctor of medicine is attached to the colony, but the identity of this person has never been fully determined.

15. Since ordinary Japanese were not allowed surnames until at least 1875, the fact that so many of the people on the U.S. census list only have one name is evidence of their commoner/farmer background. One cannot deduce the status of people with two names—were they samurai?

16. *Daily Alta California*, August 6, 1871.

17. *Daily Morning Call*, January 1–3, 1870.

Chapter Five

The Wakamatsu Dream

A Diverse and Flourishing Agricultural Community

The pioneers from Wakamatsu who came to California had dreams of building a flourishing agricultural colony that would provide a livelihood for one hundred or more of their compatriots. John Henry Schnell told a San Francisco newspaper that they hoped to have a working farm that would employ as many as four hundred Japanese colonists. They envisioned the production of tea and silk to a supposedly eager California public who would hopefully demand these goods that until then had been major exports from Japan. The Japanese farmers hoped also to grow rice for their own consumption and for sale. They had plans for other crops as well as the production of fish in a man-made lake that they planned to construct.[1]

At least in theory their plans were practical. During the 1850s, gold mining was the chief preoccupation of many newly minted Californians. There were the miners themselves as well as many others who made a living selling the miners the food and tools they would need to continue their mining. By the early 1860s, however, the mining industry had subsided and the search began for other ways to make a living. The new state government became a strong supporter of the widespread transformation of the economy from one based on mining to agriculture and to industries such as the production of silk.

Many Californians began to see vast potential in agriculture. There had to be a large truck farming industry to supply the public with basic fruits and vegetables, but the construction of the transcontinental railway connecting California to the Midwest and East in the 1860s gave Californians the idea that they should produce agricultural products that could be sent to the large markets of the East. Although locally grown vegetables would never survive the trip to the East, nonperishable goods like tea, silk, and cotton might do quite well. There was also an early start to the wine industry. The owner of the farm and land who sold his property to John Henry Schnell had grown a great variety of grapes and made wine and other spirits that he sold to the miners. Thus, Schnell and his Japanese considered bottling wine and exporting it to Japan.

Even before the arrival of the Wakamatsu Japanese, there was a major statewide effort to create a vast silk industry in California. A French producer of silk came to California during this period, preaching the idea that California was better suited than France for the growth of a sericulture industry. The California State Legislature adopted a program that would pay a bounty of $250 for every farmer who had a plantation of five thousand mulberry trees at least two years old and $300 for one hundred thousand merchantable cocoons produced. These bounties encouraged the planting of trees and the production of cocoons. According to one report in 1869, there were over ten million mulberry trees in various stages of growth in central and southern California, which in turn almost bankrupted the state government. However, a severe drought in 1869–1870 and a lack of any palpable demand for the cocoons led to a sudden downturn in the silk industry by 1871.[2]

There was also considerable interest in promoting the production of tea in California. The presence of imports of Japanese and Chinese tea unloaded at San Francisco and sent by rail to the East coast as of 1869 suggested to many Californians that their state could benefit from the production of tea, especially Chinese and Japanese teas. There was also a bounty offered by the state government to those farmers who would attempt the cultivation of tea plants. However, both the silk and tea bounties were rescinded by the state legislature in 1870.[3]

A contemporary newspaper, the *Daily Alta California*, reported in 1869 an even wilder experiment with the idea of producing silk. It stated that the state bounty on producing mulberry trees had led to the growth of over eighty million mulberry trees in California, at least half of them in nurseries. The successful production of this many trees would be sufficient to feed a large number of silkworms, but the quality of many of the trees was poor—at least half of them had to be replanted or thrown away.

The newspaper questioned the efficacy of the bounty. It was certainly a stimulus to the nursery business, but attracted thousands of people eager to collect money from the state but who had absolutely no intention of entering the silk business. There was no evidence of anyone willing to invest in the actual production of silk, which would start with machinery for silk reeling. There was some talk of exporting silk cocoons to the eastern United States, but freight rates were far too high to make that enterprise worthwhile.[4]

Subsequent California newspapers reported a series of disasters to the state's infant silk industry in July 1869 just as Schnell and the Japanese were getting settled. The *California Farmer and Journal of Useful Sciences* of July 22, 1869, wrote that several major producers of silkworms in the state had reported a total loss of their worms because heated air had entered their silkworms' cocoons, thereby decimating the entire worm population. This destruction of their silkworms had forced several of California's leading silkworm producers out of business, thus putting the entire state's experiment with silk in grave danger of collapse.[5]

Some other Californians had the bright idea of growing cotton for export to Asia and to the East. The Civil War had caused great destruction in the production of cotton in the South, and the hope was that California might take advantage of this deficit. It is said that in the mid-1860s much of the land in and around Los Angeles was given over to the production of cotton. Whether or not there were many textile businesses in California at the time that used the locally grown cotton is not clear, but if any existed, they were not in great enough demand to merit the growth of local cotton. Unfortunately for California, the production of cotton revived very quickly in the South, further impeding the California cotton industry.[6]

The brief but intense surge in the growth of mulberry trees and the production of cocoons coincided exactly with the inception of the Wakamatsu colony in Coloma. The belief that California could become a major center for the production of silk and even tea might well have intrigued the colonists and helped to inspire the creation of the farm. By the late 1860s Japan was known for its production of silk and tea, both of which were nationwide occupations that Japanese moving to other countries could readily take with them.

The large bounty paid by the state may well have attracted the attention of John Henry Schnell, but if California lacked any equipment for silk reeling, one must wonder how the folks at Gold Hill could have actually produced finished silk. They brought plenty of mulberry trees, which they proposed to plant soon after their arrival in California, but oddly there is no mention of any silk reeling equipment essential to the process in producing silk.

JAPAN'S EXPORTS AND THE NATIONAL ECONOMY DURING THE MEIJI ERA

Building a national economy was one of the key aims of Japan's new Meiji government. The goal was to introduce Western industry to Japan. At first the Japanese government played a significant role in the development of key industries such as ship building, but by the 1880s the government began selling off its factories to private companies that worked hand-in-hand with the government to develop modern industries in Japan.

Purchasing Western goods led to a massive growth of imports throughout the Meiji period (1868–1912). There was an immense demand for industrial goods from the West and initially no real demands for Japanese goods, but that was soon to change. The fact that the "Unequal Treaties" with Western powers forced Japan to set low tariff rates of 5 percent for Western imports led to a cascade of American and European goods entering Japan. Cheap cotton textiles from Great Britain flooded into Japan during the 1870s, forcing a great decline in Japan's traditional textile industry. Japan quickly faced a trade deficit, which required finding products that Japan could sell to the West to provide the Japanese with enough foreign currency to buy necessary foreign goods.[7]

Over time Japan began to sell a wide variety of goods to the West and to other nations in Southeast Asia and elsewhere. At first it was exceedingly difficult for Japanese businesses to find markets where they could compete successfully against American and European enterprises. Some Japanese businesses resorted to trying to capture foreign markets by selling their products at a loss as a way of achieving higher market share, but they were unable to sustain these practices indefinitely.

It took a while, but by the 1870s Japanese businesses found that one industry where they could compete successfully at a profit was in silk. Later in the Meiji period, when Japanese businesses decided to enter the international market for silk, a massive blight had struck down the large silk industry in Italy. The failure of the Italian silk supply resulted in higher prices for its silk in both North America and Europe. This calamity for Italy opened the door for Japanese silk producers to make a comfortable profit. Silk remained an important export item for Japan well into the early twentieth century. The Japanese produced an average of 1,026 tons of silk in 1868–1872 (646 tons for export); 1,687 tons in 1883 (1,347 tons for export); and 12,460 tons average in 1909–1913 (9,460 tons for export).[8]

Tea was also an important commodity for export. When foreigners arrived in Japan in the 1860s in greater numbers, one of the things that they appreciated was drinking Japanese green tea. It attracted so much attention that Japanese green tea was one of the highlights of the 1876 Centennial Exhibition in Philadelphia, where there was a section featuring goods from Japan. Many Americans took a great liking to the tea, which was said to have many desirable qualities including good health to the frequent imbiber. The export of tea began in earnest in the late 1860s reaching 7,388 tons of tea exported—an astounding 94.7 percent of Japan's total tea production. Exports kept growing at a steady pace, so much so that in 1899, 20,839 tons were exported, about three-quarters of Japan's total production.[9]

When Yokohama opened as one of Japan's key export terminals in 1859, tea exports were sent in almost equal amounts to Great Britain, continental Europe, and the United States. However, after the American Civil War, the

United States had become the largest market anywhere for Japanese tea. For the rest of the nineteenth century, the United States purchased between 80 to 90 percent of all of Japan's tea exports. During much of this period, tea accounted for close to 25 percent of Japan's total export trade.[10]

Silkworm egg sheets, which could produce silkworm cocoons, and raw silk, however, were even more important than tea for Japan's growing export trade. During the latter part of the 1800s Japan's silk export trade became an increasingly important element in Japan's overall economic development. It is estimated that silk exports constituted a third of Japan's total export trade from the late 1860s through the early 1920s. The Aizu domain and Wakamatsu had been a major silk-producing area since the 1700s, so many of its residents were very familiar with the process of producing raw silk.[11]

Demand for these and other Japanese goods helped to reduce the trade gap and to bring Japan badly needed foreign currency. But it also strengthens the rationale behind Schnell's conception of the Wakamatsu Farm Colony: if demand for these goods was so high in the United States, would it not be cheaper and more convenient to produce these goods there?

THE WAKAMATSU COLONY'S PLAN FOR AGRICULTURE

It is difficult to determine what the long-term plans were for the Wakamatsu colony farmers because they left no written records, but it is clear that their initial goal was to build a farm complex that could produce both tea and silk, items that were in real demand in California and the United States as a whole. The initial party from Aizu brought substantial supplies with them. Before leaving Japan, Schnell acquired a large cargo of agricultural goods that included fifty thousand three-year-old mulberry trees, a considerable supply of silkworms, bamboo, wax trees, six million tea plant seeds, and rice, citrus, and other Japanese crops. All these goods were to be used to start their Japanese tea and silk farm.[12]

When the *Daily Alta California*, published its lengthy article on June 16, 1869, upon the arrival of Schnell, his wife and daughter, and the six Japanese colonists who accompanied them to California, the author of the article enthusiastically summarized the agricultural plans and goals of the Wakamatsu colony:

> The Graynor Ranch, now Adzu Ranch, just bought by Herr Schnell, for the Japanese colony, is on the Georgetown Stage Road, four and a half miles from Placerville. The land is best adapted to fine silk and tea which they have come to cultivate. The land includes a large orchard of trees, grape bearing vines not needing irrigation, plenty of grain fields in good crops, a good brick house well furnished, a well-appointed wine house, implements of husbandry,

horses, wagons, cows, pigs, fowls and so on, all for $5000. Water is good and abundant for irrigation.[13]

The land would be divided and each family would farm its own piece of land. There would be cottages for each family of colonists who came from Japan. Each family would have its own garden and would be responsible for planting and caring for tea and the production of raw silk on its own lot. Each family would feed its own silkworms and spin its own cocoons. They would then join other colonists in sending their produce to market and would be paid according to the quantity and quality of their silk. This raises the question of whether the Japanese workers might be considered as individual contractors or as simple wage workers.

Tea would be made following the same principles. The colonists would cultivate the tea plants, pick the leaves, and send them to the "factory" where the tea would be processed for sale. There would also be a nursery where a variety of Japanese plants and trees, not well known in California, would be sold.[14] The newspaper noted that under ideal conditions in Japan, tea flourished best in a climate where there were at least sixty days of frost and coverage of snow. According to the *Sacramento Daily Union* of June 19, 1869, only a few days after Schnell and his initial party had arrived at Gold Hill, Schnell made the decision to focus first on the production of tea rather than silk. Silk production was a much more difficult enterprise to jump start, while tea was far easier to produce and was judged to be much more profitable than silk, at least during the early stages of the colony. Only days after their arrival at their new home the colonists began to plant their tea seedlings in the soil near their barn.[15] A report in the *Daily Alta California* two weeks later on July 3, 1869, suggests that the colonists were planting mulberry tree seedlings as well as seeds for tea plants, but that Mr. Schnell was especially interested in generating an early tea crop as a means of making money.[16]

An article appearing in the *Daily Alta California* on July 30, 1869, reported a visit by one or more of the newspaper's reporters to the Japanese colony. He was met by an enthusiastic John Henry Schnell, who showed him around the site of the tea plantings. After only a few weeks, the seedlings were coming up and in only a few weeks were one or two inches tall. Schnell said that this was a much faster rate of growth than one would experience in Japan. The soil and weather conditions in California were excellent. He noted that tea grew best in hilly climates that had up to two months of snow cover each winter. One must wonder if Schnell understood that there is very little snow in the Gold Hill and Coloma region.[17]

The Colony's optimism early in the summer, however, seems to have declined by autumn. One or more journalists from the *Sacramento Daily Union* journeyed to Gold Hill in mid-September to see how the Colony was faring. What they found shocked them. They had expected to see a large number of Japanese working there—Schnell had told journalists in late May and early June that more Japanese workers and their families were on their way—but they only saw a small group. To be fair, a larger group of Japanese workers did arrive the next month to join the original party.

The journalist was also shocked to find the tea plants and the mulberry trees faring very badly. Many of both had been planted earlier in the summer, but the dry weather and other negative conditions had killed virtually everything that the colonists had attempted to grow. The journalist's conclusion was that Schnell had produced a lot of hype about the colony, but that the truth was that their experiment was experiencing hard times. The following is the report he published in the September 18, 1869, issue of the *Sacramento Daily Union*:

> In a former letter I spoke of the Japanese colony located at Gold Hill several months ago, and gave items as I received them, in part from Schnell, the agent, but more generally from those who were intimate with them,—and who, from their business relation, with the colony, I thought I could rely upon what they said. Circumstances have of late shown that my informants were deceived, or, if not, they deceived others. There are but eight Japanese, four males and the same number of females, and it is not known that any more are on their way here. The 140 reported at the time of the arrival of those now here, soon to arrive, never embarked from their native country. From what I can learn it looks as if the thing would be a "fizzle." Yet we all hope their efforts will be crowned with success.
>
> Of the several millions of tea seeds brought and planted by the colony less than 180 plants have been produced, and they are in a puny condition; besides, only two of the fine mulberry trees of the several hundred brought are alive, not having been able to withstand the dry summer. The President of the State Agricultural Society must have been deceived also; or he would not have incorporated the following into his address delivered at the Pavilion on the 7th: Experiments in tea culture, now being made in El Dorado county, by a large company of Japanese, who have immigrated to our State for that purpose within the last year, are giving evidences of success beyond all expectation. The plants, set out under most disadvantageous circumstances, late in the season, are growing much better than in Japan, and the question of whether the successful production of tea in all our foothills is fully settled already—the only question remaining to be decided being the quality of the tea produced, and the experiment so far gives good indication of a favorable answer to this question.[18]

A month later the *Daily Alta California* published an article that included the contents of a letter from John Henry Schnell in which he angrily refuted the charges made against the colony in the September 18 article noted above. Schnell stated that his crops of tea and mulberry trees were growing, that the colony was here to stay, and that thirteen new workers had arrived from

Japan, which in turn would lead to the expansion of the Colony's agricultural endeavors.[19]

OTHER AGRICULTURAL PURSUITS

In addition to its main products, the colony also had plans to develop a variety of other enterprises with the goal of becoming as self-sufficient as possible Later on when everybody got settled and the farm was up and in operation, the colonists said that their plan was to produce grapes for wine making. Wine making was to be another important activity of the colony, but not right away. The Graner family had planted a substantial vineyard and sold both wine and brandy to local miners, but since wine from grapes was not a tradition in Japan, the colonists would have to learn how to make wine. The hope was that they could develop forms of wine that would meet the tastes of their own countrymen and that they could find a market for their wine in Japan. Wine would be the one product that they would export back to Japan.[20] Unfortunately, the colonists had no experience in wine making in Japan. It is probable that the colonists would have learned the art of wine making, and perhaps even the art of making brandy, but alas their tenure in El Dorado County was far too short and they really never got around to making it.

Another intended side industry was the production of bamboo. The bamboo plant would produce bounteous shoots that would combine with the culinary virtues of the artichoke and asparagus. Bamboo shoots were said to be "more marrowy and delicious" than either California vegetable.

In addition, colonists planned a lake constructed for fish cultivation. According to the *Daily Alta California* of June 16, 1869:

> The very first day those people laid out a lake for fish culture on their new purchase, there being water and a well-adapted spot among the undulations of the land. Fish grow to great size under protection from devouring enemies. The carp attains a length of not infrequently, five feet. Of all human food fish is the least trouble to cultivate and being always fat and succulent in these enclosures, the meat is exceptionally nutritious. To make such lakes hold water, the Japanese form a cheap and effective cement by a simple mixture of shell-lime, sand and ashes.[21]

Rice would also be grown to feed the colonists but would not necessarily be used for sale on the open market. It would be a special form of rice grown in Japan which thrives on higher mountain slopes and not the lowland variety, also common to Japan, which would not be appropriate for the foothills of the Sierra Nevada where Coloma is located. There is no evidence that the

Wakamatsu Colony ever made a concerted effort to grow rice and it took until 1908 for any California farmer to successfully produce rice.[22]

Access to water for irrigation was and today remains an important factor in farming this land. The lack of rain during a very dry, hot summer hampered the Colony's crops, and later when they used water from a mining ditch, the water was contaminated by trace minerals from mining. The result was the ruination of the first tea crop.

REPORTS OF SUCCESS AND FAILURE

Whether the farm colony was doing well or marching toward failure depended on the eyes of the visiting journalist in late July 1869. An anonymous writer for the *Daily Alta California* wrote a glowing portrait of the Wakamatsu farmers:

> The Japanese are intelligent as we are. They are brave, industrious and economical. They have a sort of cooperative principal which maintains the dignity of labor and takes away its subservience. They will win universal respect by a sort of heathenish habit they have of minding their own business.[23]

Soon after their arrival at Coloma in June 1869, the colonists rushed to set up their operation. It was essential to start the cultivation of the land and the preparation of crops. They quickly planted mulberries, tangerines, Koshu grapes, and tea. Reports in various papers indicate that six weeks after the tea seedlings were planted, they were "all up to a finger' height." Schnell and perhaps some Japanese attended the State Agricultural Fair later in the summer of 1869 where they displayed "very large and fine cocoons, *morus alba japonica* mulberry and oil plants." Editors from the nearby Placerville *Mountain Democrat* came to inspect the Japanese colony at Gold Hill and told the world that the tea plants were in "vigorous health." The mulberry trees were also growing well, "perfectly healthy in appearance. The oil plants had supposedly "found their element in both soil and climate. Silkworms raised at the farm were "much larger and of a brighter color than the ordinary silkworm."[24]

A full year after their arrival, Schnell and two of the Japanese colonists attended the annual Horticultural Fair in San Francisco. While there, they put on "a fine display of Japanese plants, grown from imported shrubs and seeds."[25] Initially, the Wakamatsu Tea and Silk Colony seemed quite successful. According to an article published in the *San Francisco Call* in 1870 after the Horticultural Fair in San Francisco in June:

> Herr Schnell of the Japanese Colony in Gold Hill, El Dorado County makes a fine display of Japanese plants, grown from imported shrubs and seeds. Amongst his articles are fine healthy tea plants, which were planted on March

14, 1870 last. These plants are about four inches high and are vigorous and healthy. He also exhibited samples of rice plants and a specimen of the Japanese pepper tree.

The news from the colony seemed so promising that an agricultural expert from California, one Eugene Van Reed, sent an agricultural expert to Yokohama to determine for himself which plants could be sent from Japan to California for a profit. He brought back a variety of plants and samples of different kinds of rice that might flourish in California. He also determined that he had encountered a great number of Japanese who were waiting to learn of the success or failure of the colony. If it proved successful, they would also emigrate in search of a new life in California.[26]

The newspaper reports providing a continuing flow of assessments on the success or failure of tea production at the colony were sometimes optimistic and at other times less so. Journalist K. W. Lee reports that, as late as the 1870 winter, the U.S. surveyor general, who had personally inspected the ranch, reported in *The Union* that the tea-growing project wasn't "a failure," although many tea plants had perished under prolonged drought. "I look upon these seedlings as the basis of a most important export for this state." Of the 175,000 mulberry plants, the surveyor observed, the colony was already raising cocoons and silkworm eggs. Upland rice, he added, had "a good crop this year . . . really a most valuable addition to our stock of grains."[27]

A correspondent for the *Daily Morning Call,* who visited the farm colony in early January 1870, had written:

> Here I saw, for the first time in my life, the tea-plant in growth. From the experiments thus far made, Mr. Schnell is convinced that the problem of tea culture in California is solved, and there is no longer doubt but as we can raise as good teas here as are produced in China and Japan. The few plants which I saw were only an experimental crop, planted in July [1869], when the ground was dry, hard and parched, raised under the most disadvantageous circumstances, in one of the driest seasons ever known, but show all the signs of a healthy and vigorous condition.[28]

So by these accounts, grape and wine production, fish farming, and the cultivation of rice and bamboo—along with the produce from privately tended vegetable gardens and orchards—would eventually supplement the Wakamatsu Colony's primary industries of silk and tea production. Sketched out in this way, each proposed enterprise sounds viable. Taken as a whole, they promote a vision of the Wakamatsu Colony Farm as a multifaceted enterprise, not wholly dependent on a single commodity, whose workers would prosper from an enviable balance between their own individual labors and the pooling of resources and markets by the collective whole.

Schnell and his Japanese crew worked diligently to create a viable enterprise, and they showed signs of making real progress, but its ultimate success depended on a growing number of workers, adequate funding, and ample rainfall, but ultimately none of these factors came into play. Above all they needed time to develop their crops and to generate some income, but sadly they ran out of time before they could record some measurable successes.

It is important to note that despite its ultimate failure, the Colony successfully planted America's first known crops of tea. Their early success in this and other endeavors gained public attention and won some awards. It is said that these endeavors ultimately failed, but as some contemporary journalists noted, the Colony demonstrated the feasibility of growing Japanese tea and other crops in California under better conditions.

Today all that is left of the colonists' endeavors is a huge keyaki (Japanese elm) tree in the yard of the restored farmhouse.

NOTES

1. *Daily Alta California*, May 27, 1869.
2. J. M. Guinn, "Some Early California Industries That Failed," *Annual Publication of the Historical Society of Southern California*, July 1907, 3–7.
3. Guinn, "Some Early California Industries."
4. "Silk Manufactures in California," *Daily Alta California*, May 21, 1869.
5. "Calamity to the Silk Worms," *California Farmer and Journal of Useful Sciences*, July 22, 1869.
6. Guinn, "Some Early California Industries," 3–7. Guinn in his article goes to great lengths to describe other experiments that failed. He tells how a Col. Hollister of Santa Barbara County planted a small forest of tea trees in his county and even went as far as importing Japanese tea farmers to manage the crop. The experiment involved a lot of intensive labor, and Hollister found that the prices he charged for his tea were equal to or higher than tea imports. A speculator farmer had the idea of growing coffee trees in San Bernardino. Although the climate and soil proved ideal for the production of coffee, California coffee was more expensive than imports from Central America. Another failed experiment was an attempt to grow Caster Beans. Guinn speculates that the reason that these products were so expensive was the lack of cheap labor.
7. Unequal treaty is the name given by the Chinese to a series of treaties during the nineteenth and early twentieth centuries by Qing dynasty China and late Tokugawa Japan after suffering military defeat by the foreign powers or when there was a threat of military action by those powers. These treaties brought severe limitations on the sovereignty of both China and Japan in that both nations lost the right to regulate foreign trade and tariffs on foreign goods. These treaties with Japan remained in force until the 1890s and early 1900s.
8. http://www.sjsu.edu/faculty/watkins/meiji.htm (accessed September 1, 2018)
9. https://japaneseteasommelier.wordpress.com/2012/04/14/when-japanese-tea-shone-in-the-world-the-development-and-export-of-sencha-1853-1918/
10. John E. Van Sant, *Pacific Pioneers: Japanese Journeys to America and Hawaii, 1850–80* (Urbana and Chicago: University of Illinois Press, 2000), 123.
11. Van Sant, *Pacific Pioneers*, 123.
12. "Arrival of Japanese Immigrants," *Daily Alta California*, May 27, 1869.
13. *Daily Alta California*, June 16, 1869.
14. *Daily Alta California*, June 16, 1869.
15. Letter from Placerville, *Sacramento Daily Union*, June 19, 1869.

16. "The Japanese Colony and Tea Culture," *Daily Alta California*, July 3, 1869.
17. "The Japanese Colony," *Daily Alta California*, July 30, 1869.
18. "The Japanese Colony," *Sacramento Daily Union*, September 18, 1869.
19. *Daily Alta California*, October 24, 1869.
20. *Daily Alta California*, July 30, 1869.
21. It is unclear whether the Wakamatsu colonists ever constructed this fish pond. Also there is no palpable record of fish being brought into the Colony. In other words, the pond was certainly another pipe dream. Today there is a substantial pond above the farm, but it was created by the Veerkamp family long after the Japanese had gone, only in 1908.
22. *Daily Alta California*, June 16, 1869. Early records indicate a strong effort to grow rice in California as far back as 1856. Attempts were made to grow rice in the water-rich San Joaquin Valley. When that failed, rice paddies were tried as far afield as Redding and the Los Angeles area. While some farmers could get the plants to grow, the grain never formed. Finally by 1908, a short-grained rice called Kiushu planted in the northern Sacramento Valley thrived. See Tim Johnson, "Rice in California: The Japanese Connection," unpublished manuscript.
23. *Daily Alta California*, June 16, 1869.
24. Van Sant, *Pacific Pioneers*, 126.
25. Van Sant, *Pacific Pioneers*, 126.
26. *Daily Alta California*, October 24, 1869.
27. K. W. Lee, "Gold Hill Colony: Hope and Betrayal for a 'Mayflower,'" *Nichi Bei Times*, January 1, 2011.
28. *Daily Morning Call*, January 1, 1870.

Chapter Six

The Last Days of the Wakamatsu Tea and Silk Colony Farm

Despite its early apparent success the Wakamatsu Farm Colony soon endured a number of crises that combined led to its very swift collapse by the early summer of 1871. We saw in the last chapter that tea and silk were popular commodities being discussed by leaders of California's agricultural industry. Strong demand for Asian, particularly Japanese, silk and tea and the May 1869 completion of a transcontinental railroad convinced many Californians that a great future lay ahead in the production of tea and silk with a wide open market in the East. Despite this interest, neither product ultimately succeeded in becoming a dominant force in California's agricultural economy.

It is unfortunate that we have so little information on the management, distribution of labor, or even the daily operation of the Colony Farm. We do not know anything about John Henry Schnell's ability as a farm manager. He was still a young man not yet thirty when he and the initial group of Japanese arrived at Golden Hill in June 1869. There is little to indicate whether Schnell had any experience as a farmer, but since he brought Japanese farmers and carpenters with him, perhaps he was able to rely on their expertise to make a go at it.

John Henry Schnell was an ambitious businessman who gambled on the notion that with luck and good planning, his venture at Gold Hill might succeed. Early success might build on itself, attracting customers in California and further recruits from Japan who would make Wakamatsu Farm a flourishing Japanese colony. Bounties offered by the state of California might provide enough funding to keep the dream alive. Sadly, a prolonged drought in 1870, coupled with a tainted water supply, a lack of capital and investors, and the departure of many of the Japanese workers sank the enterprise before it ever got going.

Schnell and his colleagues reached the high point of their endeavor at the start of September 1870 at the annual agricultural fair held at the Pavilion in San Francisco. According to the *Daily Alta California*,[1] the exposition was a very competitive event with highly desired awards going to the participant with the best commodity in many fields. Prizes for the best wines produced in California garnered most of the attention, but there were plenty of other prize-winning categories.

The *Daily Alta California* listed Schnell as a winner in four categories, including the best specimen of a tea plant as well as prizes for specimens of mountain rice plant, a goma (sesame) plant, and a pepper plant. Schnell and the Wakamatsu Colony won good publicity by winning these competitions and having their prizes listed in one of the leading California newspapers of the time.

John Henry Schnell, his Japanese wife Jou, and their two baby daughters climbed into a wagon at Gold Hill sometime in early June 1871, almost two years since his family, as well as an advance group of Japanese, had arrived at their newly purchased farm. By the time that Schnell and his family departed, many if not most of the Japanese workers had already left.[2] The dream of building a vibrant Japanese colony died with no hope of resurrection. It is said that Schnell told those he left behind that he hoped to go to Japan to secure more money, supplies, and workers, but he and his family disappeared into oblivion.

Schnell's departure drew some attention in the California press. There was a consensus that Schnell's agricultural pursuits had been successful, but that a combination of other factors ultimately defeated him. It is instructive to read contemporary press accounts to assess their opinions of what Schnell had demonstrated about the potential of tea cultivation in California and why his own experiment had ultimately failed.

The *Pacific Rural Press* (1871–1922) was California's leading farm magazine at the turn of the last century. A special issue published on February 15, 1879, devoted to "Tea Culture in California" included a short article on the Japanese colony at Gold Hill:[3]

> Tea Culture in California.
>
> A contemporary, usually correct in his pronouncements concerning the California economy, has been led into conveying an erroneous impression about tea culture in this State. Herr Schnell, with his 22 Japanese people, proved, in cultivating over a million of plants, and in making some tea therefrom, that the tea plant finds every favorable condition of soil and climate along the whole line of our Nevada foothills. His experiment was a success agriculturally, as recorded in the transactions of our Agricultural Society. He made a small box of tea to satisfy friends; and though the plants were not ripe for plucking, the beverage was like Japan tea in flavor.

An unlooked for casualty destroyed his tea plants when in full vigor of growth. This swamped him financially and beyond recovery. The casualty, which cannot occur again, was in this wise. Summer irrigation is required; and he used the miner's water from the public zanga. The water was allowed to be in contact with the plants. All mine water holds iron and sulphur in suspension. The growing plants having affinity for those elements, a ring was precipitated around each plant, near the ground. Thus was every plant throttled, its bark cut through, and all perished.

The "I told you so" neighbors trumpeted "failure;" "California won't grow tea." Let this narrative correct the false impression. The same paper makes another mistake. It conveys the impression that no tea plant is at present to be found in the State, to prove that the plant will ever come to perfection in this climate. Hundreds of tea plants are growing in our State—proving exactly the reverse of this declaration.

The most thorough analysis of the collapse of the Wakamatsu colony came in a long article in the *Daily Alta California* on August 6, 1871. Like the later piece in the *Pacific Rural Press,* this local article focuses on irrigation problems facing the Colony, but there is also a discussion of labor problems which caused many of the Japanese workers to leave the farm weeks before Schnell's own departure:[4]

"Failure Analysis"

Regarding the probability of raising tea in California, we have only theory to guide us. Herr Schnell tried it on a large scale near Placerville last year, without success. The soil is reddish strains, usually considered best. The tea seed sprouted well; the young plants from Japan made an excellent growth at first, but they finally died out.

The failure may perhaps be referred to other causes than want of adaptability to our soil and climate. That others may not be discouraged, it is necessary to reveal some personal history which otherwise we should not ventilate. Herr Schnell, a Prussian gentleman, was long resident among the tea gardens of Northern Japan, where he married a beautiful and accomplished native lady and became master of many Retainers skilled in tea making. It is customary for "Retainers" to follow their master and look to him for support. On account of revolutionary troubles, Herr Schnell came here, followed by over twenty retainers, with whom he made contracts which would warrant him in going into raising tea in California.

His experts pronounced the foothills safe for tea planting. He bought a large preempted farm at a very low price, and the miners' ditch offered irrigation at a very small figure. Everything appeared favorable, and the millions of seed and young plants made a brilliant first success. The soil proved very thirsty, but water was plenty.

Something began to wither the young trees. It was caused by a deposition from the running water, which girdled the saplings with a metallic ring near the ground, and choked the life out of them. It was iron and sulphur. This necessitated expensive conduction of other far-off water, which came too late for salvation.

The Japanese have much savvy. They found out something about the right of revolution and of the invalidity of contracts for personal service. Four dollars a month began to disturb them; the neighboring workmen incited them to stampede. To hire labor at going rates, to keeping a plantation, would cost more by double than the production would cover. And this ended the enterprise, leaving the estimable proprietor with an exhausted exchequer and a broken spirit to make a scant living in a strange land for his devoted wife and children.

It is to be hoped that some association may yet be found to renew the experiment and to avail of Herr Schnell's knowledge in the premises. From this truthful narration, it will be seen that nothing indicates unfavorably to tea culture in California, except the matter of labor, against which we have the hope that American ingenuity will contrive machinery to cheapen cultivation and leaf gathering, and possibly to perfect the manufacture as well as to reduce its expenses.

Another experiment, of more recent date, is being made at Calistoga.[5] None of our agricultural societies and none of our farm journals seem to take interest in this experiment for they make no note of its progress. We cannot even get information from disinterested visitors at Calistoga. Yet, we believe the enterprise has no small proportions. It has the superintendence of a skilled Japanese workman and ample irrigation.

An article that appeared in the *Pacific Rural Press* on April 15, 1871, speaks strongly for government assistance for people like Schnell who were endeavoring to introduce new crops and products to the California economy. The magazine supports a special law passed in Congress to give Schnell an opportunity to pay only $1.25 per acre for an additional 640 acres of public land to expand his operations. They point out that starting a business like the Wakamatsu colony is a very expensive endeavor, far too expensive for any one individual. The government had offered some subsidies to people willing to set up a tea or silk production business, but that subsidy had been discontinued in 1870:[6]

Protection to Silk and Tea Culture

The land upon which Herr Schnell and his Japanese colony developed for the cultivation of tea and silk was located in El Dorado County, and was unsurveyed public land. This fact has been the source of great annoyance and discouragement to the colony; so much so that the originators of the enterprise had almost lost heart to continue the experiment. The friends of the industrial progress of the State will be gratified that this annoyance is now at an end. Through the instrumentality of Capt. John Mullen of this city and Congressman Sargent, a special law has been passed by Congress allowing Schnell to locate 640 acres, including the improvements and plantations of tea and mulberries, at $1.25 per acre. This is a just and very important law; and now our

State should aid Mr. Schnell to give the matter a thorough and satisfactory trial. No one man should be called upon to defray alone the expense, and assume the risk of so costly and important an undertaking. The law offering premiums on tea and silk and which was an inducement for Mr. Schnell to come here and engage in their culture was repealed by the last Legislature. Justice to the colony and the best interests of the State should dictate that the promises held out by that law should be redeemed or at least, that such aid should be extended, as is necessary to give tea culture a thorough and satisfactory trial in the State.

THE END OF A NOBLE EXPERIMENT

There can be no doubt that the noble experiment to create a viable farm producing tea, silk, and other agricultural products ended in failure. The *Idea* of creating a tea and silk farm made perfect sense. There was strong demand for Japanese silk and tea in the United States, and these commodities constituted a significant share of Japan's exports to the United States and Europe throughout the last four decades of the nineteenth century. The idea of having Japanese producing these products in the United States and Canada had never been tried before. It was widely known that the state of California was attempting to jumpstart a silk-producing industry, but without much success. Producing silk and tea in North America would avoid long trans-Pacific travel costs, middlemen, and tariffs.

Schnell's decision to focus on tea and silk makes it clear that he was well aware of these inducements. Furthermore, the crushing defeat of the Aizu domain meant that he was unemployed and that he had to quickly find a new line of work away from Japan. There were plenty of workers in Aizu with experience in growing tea, producing silk, and performing carpentry whose livelihoods had been destroyed by the complete slash-and-burn tactics of the imperial army. They were all looking to reorient their lives, so Schnell's proposal to move them to a prosperous new land far away from the turmoil of the Boshin War might sound ideal. Schnell may have been a gambler and risk-taker, and starting such a colony in a prosperous new land might well prove a worthwhile gamble.

Schnell apparently bought plenty of tools and supplies, and he seems to have carefully chosen workers who had experience in farming, tea cultivation, and silk production. He went to great lengths to take these goods and workers out of Japan. When Schnell and his first party arrived in San Francisco, Schnell acted with great alacrity in finding a plot of farmland and moving his group there in just two weeks—they arrived in late May and had moved into the former Graner farm by early to mid-June. They had planted their tea shrubs by early July.

Schnell appears to have been a bit of an opportunist and showman-publicist who knew how to handle the press. He gave American journalists the impression that his farm operation was the first wave of hundreds more Japanese who would join his colony once it was fully established and operational. Upon arrival in California in May 1869 Schnell made the suggestion that the "prince" of Aizu would come to live there in due course. This statement raises the question of the actual role that the *daimyo* Matsudaira played in the creation of the Colony. American journalists had the impression from Schnell that Matsudaira was an active supporter of the enterprise, but there is no proof one way or the other. Matsudaira was in prison or recently released when Schnell first arrived in California. Thus, even if he wanted to support Schnell in any way, that was no longer possible.

Later Schnell took samples of his tea to expositions in Sacramento and San Francisco, giving any interested parties the strong impression that his farm operation was flourishing and that the Japanese had a great future in California agriculture. The truth, however, was probably that he had grown a few tea plants, but that most of the plants had died by the summer of 1870.

Sadly, these positive and bold projections were built on proverbial quicksand! Starting a large-scale operation like the Wakamatsu colony is never easy. It involves the careful formulation of a vision and a purpose. There must then be a carefully thought-out plan to accomplish the dream. It is clear that Schnell started out with a clear plan. He hired workers who knew about the production of tea and silk, and he brought plants and other farming goods from Japan. He arrived in California with a strong determination to get to work immediately to fulfill his dream.

Schnell soon began to run into several problems including a lack of money. Such an operation would be very expensive. If one does not have enough capital oneself, one must raise it through investments by interested parties or through massive loans. No matter where the funding comes from, there must be an adequate supply and flow of money. There must be some understanding of the land one is moving to. Where would one go? Was there a guarantee that suitable land would be found, and how much would it cost to procure this land? What about the climate? Was the climate in California suitable for the production of silk and tea? A farm with such grandiose expectations would need a large and skilled workforce. What did it take to bring together such a group, and was there enough money or other ways of rewarding the workers for their toil?

There was an almost perfect storm of things that went wrong and quickly doomed the Wakamatsu Tea and Silk Colony Farm even before it actually began.

Poor Planning: It is doubtful that Schnell had ever been to California and that he understood the climate and topography of the northern part of the state. John Henry Schnell brought over many of the essential tools and plants to commence his operation, but it appears that he was unprepared for what would be a hostile climate for the production of tea and silk.

Schnell was young and had little experience as a farmer. He was a businessman, and it is hard to determine his expertise in the area of farming. He probably hoped that the Japanese workers had a strong foundation of experience in farming to get the operation up and going. As in any venture, the person or people in charge must have a clear sense of what they are doing. One must wonder whether Schnell's lack of a background in agriculture was a factor.

Northern California was hit by one of its worst droughts in 1869–1871. Farming in California is a risky business if you do not have access to a reliable storage facility for water. There are violent swings in the weather. Rain comes from December to March. If there is considerable rain as well as snow in the high Sierras, there will be adequate water for farming, but in times of drought, those without access to adequate water face disaster. This was the case with the Wakamatsu colony. They also used iron- and sulphur-tainted water from mines detrimental to plants.

Schnell sorely lacked the financial resources to launch his operation. Buying 160 acres of land and starting a large-scale operation like that proposed by Schnell requires considerable capital. The land that Schnell required was not cheap by 1869 standards in rural California, but Schnell could only afford a 10 percent down payment. A foreclosure was the inevitable result of Schnell's lack of money.

There were no obvious investors to help finance the operation. While there is some speculation that the daimyo of Aizu, Mastudaira, gave Schnell some seed money to jump-start the colony, there is no evidence that he did so. Whatever seed money Schnell might have acquired was by no means enough.

By April 1871 a vast majority of the Japanese workers had left the farm. Schnell was not able to provide them with a living wage, so they left to seek better opportunities elsewhere. It is not clear where most of them went and what they did.

POOR PLANNING AND DROUGHT

Schnell's imagined concept of a tea- and silk-producing operation was fine, but we have no idea how long Schnell was planning this venture. The Imperial attack on the northern domains took place during the summer of 1868, but it was only a few months after Aizu had collapsed that Schnell was buying up supplies, gathering a group of workers, and setting off to California. Whether he had been thinking of creating a colony in California for a long time or not,

Schnell quickly threw together a grand scheme and tried to implement it without the key ingredients that he needed for success.

Schnell, still a fairly young man in his late twenties in 1869, probably had never been to California before and probably knew little about the history, climate, and soil conditions. He was a native German who had set off to Japan in his early twenties to seek adventure and perhaps a fortune. His military experience and background as a merchant stood him well, but to go from being an arms dealer in Japan to the proprietor of a large farm in California is a huge leap of faith. Never having been anywhere near California was a major liability. He probably did not have a deep understanding of the soil conditions and climate of California.

It is probable that Schnell was not very familiar with or prepared for the Mediterranean climate of the region. The contrast between the very moist and seasonal climate of Aizu could not have been more different. Anybody who has spent an appreciable amount of time in the foothills of the Sierra Nevada Mountains of northern California and in the mountains of northern Japan will notice a great difference in the climates of both regions. The climate of northern California varies greatly, from areas of hot desert to subarctic cold in the deep Sierra mountains, which will experience heavy snowfalls in May and June. The Central Valley and foothills of the Sierras have a Mediterranean climate with warm to hot, very dry summers and mild, moderately wet winters. There are times such as the winter of 2016–2017 when northern California gets overwhelmed with rain, but by May one can count on the fact that dry conditions will return. The High Sierras get tremendous amounts of snow in winter, but it rarely snows in the Central Valley and low foothills.

By contrast, winters in Aizu-Wakamatsu are long and cold with temperatures rising slightly above freezing during the day and slipping below freezing at night. There are long stretches of rain or snow. Conditions will improve for a stretch in late April to early June, which will feature glorious sunny days and moderate to warm temperatures. By mid-June, however, conditions change radically. A monsoon-like rainy season takes over until at least early August with moderate to heavy rain all the time save for a few quite brief stretches of drier sunny weather. The rest of August can be very hot and humid before the region experiences a cooler and drier autumn.

When I visited Gold Hill for several weeks in late May and early June 2016, northern California had experienced a moderately mild and wet 2015–2016 winter. Yet when I visited the site of the Wakamatsu farm colony on several occasions that spring and again in the fall, I found drought conditions. The soil was baked in the heat and showed a multitude of cracks. The grass throughout the property had turned a dry brown by mid-summer. Local farmers relied on groundwater for their sustenance. There is today a large pond on the property formed by a dam up behind the farmhouse, which was built later by the Veerkamp family.

The Coloma-Gold Hill region was experiencing a similar drought in the spring and summer of 1871. These arid conditions meant that the Japanese colonists could not produce much tea or many silkworm cocoons for sale in local and regional markets. Schnell and his associates had been able to sell some of the colony's agricultural products at the September 1869 State Agricultural Fair in Sacramento and again at the June 1870 Horticultural Fair in San Francisco, but there were no recorded sales of produce after that. This degree of aridity had a strong negative effect on the colony's ability to keep its tender young plants alive.[7]

Adequate irrigation is obviously an important key to the success of any farm. The Wakamatsu farm at Gold Hill is blessed with two streams that flow from the low hills up behind the farmhouse, but the main flow is in the winter, not the dry hot summer. The lack of rain probably doomed much of the Colony's crop.

CONTAMINATED WATER

Even before the summer of 1871, there were signs foreshadowing their future troubles. When rainfall appeared to be insufficient to keep the plants alive in the spring of 1871, there was a need to get water from an irrigation ditch tied to a local stream. This irrigation ditch, really a mining ditch, brought in water for some of the time, but the water itself contained iron sulfate from local gold mining. This chemical coated and strangled the surviving tea plants. According to the American River Conservancy:

> While the Wakamatsu Tea and Silk Colony thrived, the land around the colony was still being ravaged by gold seekers. There was ongoing contention between miners and the growing number of farmers and ranchers. While Schnell initially resisted irrigating crops, drought finally pushed him to purchase water from a local mining ditch. This water contained the contaminant iron sulfate which coated and ultimately killed the young plants.[8]

A terse article in the *Daily Alta California* dated July 13, 1870, and entitled "Miner Trouble" speaks of this problem. The writer reports that the Wakamatsu colony had been the target of miners who waited for Schnell and his farm laborers to lay out crops and then commenced stream mining in that area. The writer suggests ominously that the actions of the miners were perhaps influenced by racial motives, but there is little evidence to substantiate this claim. In any case, the contaminated water decimated the tea plants and other crops that the Colony was attempting to grow.

A FINANCIAL COLLAPSE AND DEPARTURE OF WORKERS

Another major problem was financial. When one actually begins an enterprise like this, it takes a while, several years in fact, to generate enough income to begin making a profit that would enable one to survive. It took a major investment to bring two dozen or more Japanese all the way to California, as well as all of the produce that they brought with them. Then there was the question of salaries to pay the workers who had come all the way from Japan.

According to the American River Conservancy:

> In addition to environmental challenges, the Colony's workforce was under a labor contract made in Japan, which paid the Japanese low wages. Schnell was running out of money and could not renegotiate with his Japanese workers who had begun to leave in search of better pay elsewhere in California. The final blow came when [the Aizu Daimyo] Matsudaira was released from captivity by the Japanese government, under the terms that he give up his wealth. The colony, desperately strapped for cash, could not hope for aid from Matsudaira.[9]

Schnell probably ran out of money sometime in late 1870 or early 1871. We have no idea how much money Schnell brought with him, but whatever the amount, it was certainly not adequate to keep the project going for very long. The major cost was the purchase of land from the Graner family, but there is no evidence beyond the original down payment of $500 that Schnell made further payments. Combined with possible financial mismanagement, the colony was unable to make further payments in 1870 on the promissory note for the land. As a result of two court rulings, the settlement's land reverted to its original owner by the spring of 1871.[10]

The situation must have looked very bleak for Schnell by the time he and his family departed the farm. He had lost title to the land, his workers had left, and his farm produce including his tea plants were in ruin. Perhaps the greatest loss was that of his workers. He had assigned them contracts in Japan to work for a salary of four dollars a month—perhaps a decent salary in Japan at the time, but wildly insufficient for the inflated cost of living in gold-rush-era California. Contemporary newspapers stated that a miner needed at least twelve dollars a month to keep going in the 1860s. One wonders whether an already bankrupt Schnell paid his workers at all in 1870 and 1871, but there are no extant records to confirm or deny this speculation. But even if Schnell had paid his workers according to their Japan contract, four dollars would not have been enough to survive in California for very long. But whatever the circumstances, a newspaper article informs us that by April 1871, many of the workers and their families had left the farm to seek work elsewhere.[11]

THE SMALL WORKFORCE

One must wonder if the workforce that Schnell brought with him was large and strong enough to adequately carry out the master plan of producing tea and silk plus other crops. Schnell only brought a small group of workers when he arrived in San Francisco in late May 1869. Two other groups of Japanese arrived in late 1869 and again in 1870. At its height there were between twenty or thirty workers including Schnell and his wife. The Colony included a number of women and a few small children who were far too young to do any meaningful farmwork. The colony also included four trained carpenters. The result is that there were only about fifteen workers to do the actual work of farming. There is no way of knowing how productive they were, but without modern tools of farming, it is possible that the workforce was too small to maintain the farm that Schnell had hoped for.

The departure of the Schnell family came simultaneously with the migration of the workers away from the Colony. We know something about a handful of the Japanese workers, but where the others went and what they did remains a mystery to this day. The carpenters would have been in greater demand than the farmworkers, and it is possible that at least two of them found employment in nearby Coloma helping to build a hotel under construction there. Others may have made their way into the recently cultivated farmland near Sacramento, but this is nothing more than mere speculation. Some eventually booked passage back to Japan, but they would have had to be very careful since their departure from Japan probably had been illegal. They would have kept a very low profile so as to not attract the attention of the authorities. Since many of the rest probably were at best semiliterate, they left no written records of their time in the United States.

Ultimately, one can say that the whole enterprise was "too little, too late." There was not enough money, too few workers, too little water, and too little time to let the tea plants mature. Schnell did succeed in an agricultural sense in demonstrating that under the right conditions Japanese tea could grow in California. One example of this is the present-day Golden Feather Tea Farm operated by Mike Fitts in California since 2010. He has experimented with processing many styles of tea which he believes are descendants of the Wakamatsu Tea and Silk Colony Farm.

One cannot build a major farm overnight without such key ingredients as labor and capital. Perhaps the ultimate benefit was the opportunity for Americans to encounter Japanese on their own land for the first time. Only a few Americans actually met the Japanese, but they were able to read about them in their California newspapers. It was most importantly the harbinger of the massive immigration of Japanese that was to begin a generation later.

EVALUATIONS OF JOHN HENRY SCHNELL AS A LEADER WHILE AT THE FARM

John Henry Schnell was certainly a courageous and charismatic leader. He was deeply attracted to Japan and went to great lengths to ingratiate himself with the Matsudaira family in Aizu. He played an important but ultimately futile role preparing the Aizu Domain to fight the imperial army. His decision to start a Japanese colony in California required both skill and determination, but he was clearly unprepared to deal with California's very different climate. Schnell and his colonists had apparently not understood the very fundamental fact that northern California's dry climate was so very different from Japan's humid one. The tea plants required good access to water. Henry Veerkamp, son of Francis Veerkamp and neighbor of the Wakamatsu Colony, recalled later that the imported plants and seedlings died to a lack of moisture.[12]

Schnell may have demonstrated good qualities as a leader and planner, but in the end his dreams were victims of a lack of funds, a prolonged drought, contaminated water, and perhaps too small a workforce. One cannot start a complex business such as this with close to thirty workers in another country without money or financial backers. As a result of two court judgments, most of the colony's land reverted to its original owner by spring 1871. Having lost his land and without any money, Schnell took his wife and two young children and abandoned the entire project and all the people involved. He promised to return, but we have no idea why he did not come back or why he disappeared. He may have been waylaid or injured or maybe he just gave up out of despair. The colony farm which he had worked so hard to create collapsed mainly due to circumstances beyond his control. Interestingly, because he owed money to the Japanese or to his neighbors the Veerkamps, Schnell left behind a silk banner as well as one *tantô* dagger with the Matsudaira family crest emblazoned on it.[13]

NOTES

1. *Daily Alta California*, September 2 and 4, 1870.
2. *Daily Alta California*, April 3, 1871.
3. "Tea Culture in California," *Pacific Rural Press*, February 15, 1879.
4. "Failure Analysis," *Daily Alta California*, August 6, 1871.
5. Calistoga is a small city in California's Napa Valley. It's known for hot springs, mud baths, and wineries, including one set in Castello di Amorosa, a medieval-style castle. The Old Faithful Geyser of California erupts at regular intervals.
6. "Protection to Silk and Tea Culture," *Pacific Rural Press*, April 15, 1871.
7. John E. Van Sant, *Pacific Pioneers: Japanese Journeys to America and Hawaii, 1850–80* (Urbana and Chicago: University of Illinois Press, 2000), 127.
8. American River Conservancy, *The Wakamatsu Tea and Silk Colony Farm: America's First Issei* (2012), 9.

9. American River Conservancy, *The Wakamatsu Tea and Silk Colony Farm*, 8.
10. Van Sant, *Pacific Pioneers*, 127.
11. *Daily Alta California*, April 3, 1871.
12. Van Sant, *Pacific Pioneers*, 127.
13. Van Sant, *Pacific Pioneers*, 128. The silk banner and dagger were recently donated to California State Parks.

Chapter Seven

The Creation of the Legendary Okei-San

Okei Ito, the young woman who came from Japan to Gold Hill probably sometime during the summer of 1870, is assuredly the most famous of the Wakamatsu colonists. Despite her fame, we know very little about her, including her youth in Aizu and the circumstances of her death at age nineteen in 1871. It seems likely that she was a nursemaid for the two infant daughters of John Henry and Jou Schnell in California. For reasons that remain unclear to this day, she remained at Gold Hill after the Schnells left, and she died from a fever-related illness not long after their departure. Okei-san disappeared from public memory at the time of her death and only reappears in the 1920s and 1930s when Japanese American historians and later a novelist and a movie producer in Japan rediscovered her. They recasted her as a mythical symbol of Japanese motherhood, a saintly Joan of Arc figure who became a symbolic beacon for future Japanese settlement both in North America and in Manchuria.

Japanese *Issei* historians rediscovered Okei-san early in the twentieth century while trying to write an inspirational history of their life experiences in California for future generations of Japanese Americans to savor. These writers saw in Okei-san the many virtues of Japanese womanhood. When they finished recreating the mythical Okei-san, she emerged as an innocent pure Japanese woman who sacrificed her life to serve as an inspiration for the thousands of Japanese who would immigrate to the United States in later years. In short, just as the mythical woman Marianne became a national symbol of the French Republic after the French Revolution—a personification of liberty and reason and a portrayal of the Goddess of Liberty—Okei-san became a personification of the virtuous Japanese heroine who created the path for the expansion of Japanese civilization abroad.

Chapter 7

THE REAL OKEI ITO

As one approaches the solitary grave of Okei Ito on a low hill overlooking the farm where she and her Japanese companions established a colony from 1869–1871, one encounters a sign with a short poem in the Japanese language, "Okei's Lullaby" standing nearby. The poem, composed by an anonymous author, captures both much of the sadness as well as romance of Okei-san's brief life and the canonization that occurred long after her death.

>Okei's Lullaby
>
>Refrain of rock-a-bye, heard in far away land,
>Okei, just seventeen, why did she cry?
>As she quietly sang the lullaby
>Of her native land, why did she cry?
>Refrain of rock-a-bye, as distant clouds swept by,
>In the lonely sunset, her heart searched afar
>Only in her dreams could she return home,
>Toward her beloved Aizu, she watched the stars.
>The song of rock-a-bye, she sang as she cried,
>Gentle Okei, longing and waiting in vain,
>As winter fled, and spring had arrived
>For glad tidings from home, which never came
>(Author anonymous. Interpreted by Henry Taketa)

Since Okei-san's name does not appear on the list of Japanese workers at Gold Hill made in June for the 1870 U.S. census, it is likely that she came with a small group of workers from Japan to join the colony sometime later that summer. Her assigned task was the care of the two baby daughters of John Henry and Jou Schnell. She may have had other household duties, but there are no existent records to document her presence during this time.

When the Schnell family left the farm in June 1871, they left behind their daughters' Japanese nanny, Okei-san, as well as one of the male workers, Sakurai Matsunosuke, who some believe had been a samurai before the fall of the Aizu domain. By then, most if not all of the other Japanese workers had left the colony in search of a better life elsewhere. The Veerkamp family took them both in and welcomed them as members of their own family. For a very short while Okei-san became a nursemaid for the many Veerkamp children while Sakurai worked on the farm. Tragically, Okei-san developed a high fever later that summer, possibly in August 1871, perhaps brought on by a severe bout of malaria, and died at the Veerkamp home. It is said that during her last summer she would on occasion wander as long as she was able to the top of a small hill on the property to watch the sun setting in the west, the direction of her home in Japan.

When Okei Ito died, she was buried on that low hill overlooking the farm house and much of the property. Sakurai later had a headstone made, which he placed at her burial spot. The 136-year-old granite headstone, inscribed in English and Japanese, reads: "In Memory of Okei, Died 1871. Aged 19 years. (A Japanese Girl)." At some point the original stone began to crack, so today an exact replica stands in its place. Okei-san's gravesite is considered the first burial spot of a Japanese woman and immigrant on American soil. Lately the grave has become a shrine of sorts for many Japanese visitors who venture there every year.

One obvious question is why the Schnell family neglected to take Okei Ito with them when they left the farm in June 1871. Schnell ostensibly claimed that he was going to Japan to get more money and supplies. Why did they make a clear decision to leave Okei-san behind? Okei-san had no particular farming skills and had no purpose for staying at the farm. The sad fact is that she was to die a short two months after the Schnells left. Thus, one wonders if Okei-san was already ill in June, too sick or infectious to go with them to help care for their daughters.

"PIONEERS OF JAPANESE DEVELOPMENT": CHRONICLING A FABRICATED PAST

By the 1920s, first generation Japanese Americans *(Issei)* were growing old and beginning to worry that the day would come when their *Nisei* children (second generation) and *Sansei* (third generation) grandchildren would know nothing about the "courageous" exploits of the pioneering generation of Japanese who paved the way for Japanese civilization in California and elsewhere. One *Issei* intellectual, Yoichi Toga, explained in the 1920s why such a historical accounting was necessary:

> A great nation / race [*minzoku*] has a [proper] historical background; a nation / race disrespectful of history is doomed to self-destruction. It has been already 70 years since we, the Japanese, marked the first step on American soil. . . . Now Issei are advancing in years, and the Nisei era is coming. . . . I believe that it is worthy of having [the second generation] inherit the record of our [immigrant] struggle against oppression and hardships, despite which we have raised our children well and reached the point at which we are now. . . . But, alas, we have very few treatises of our history to leave behind.[1]

Another *Issei* historian, writing for the benefit of the Nisei generation that was coming of age in the 1920s, urged younger Japanese Americans to better understand their history:

> To you the second generation whose whole future lies before you, and to all of our descendants in America, we wish this saga of the Japanese pioneers to be a cherished legacy to inspire you and to instill you with pride and confidence in whatever task or venture you may undertake. Then in generations to come

when our great-great-grandchildren wish to seek new worlds to conquer. . . . May the incentive provided by the stirring epic composed by their forefathers produce an atavistic recurrence of the spirit of the Japanese pioneers to guide them.[2]

These *Issei* intellectual historians were very proud of the Japanese experience in America. They had come to an alien land, had survived terrible persecution from the majority white establishment, but by the 1920s and 1930s were making important contributions to the agricultural development of California and elsewhere. The historians wanted to convey a very positive, yet unfortunately partially false, image of these Japanese pioneers. The fact that many if not most of the Japanese immigrants were uneducated and lowly men and women from some of the poorest families and regions of Japan was something they chose to ignore. The historians chose to ignore the lowly impoverished Japanese farmers and their wives and focused on virtuous women and hardworking successful and dedicated agriculturalists. They created an image of a heroic idealized version of their past.

One *Issei* writer, Shiro Fujioka, a community leader and journalist in Los Angeles, composed a treatise in Japanese in 1927 whose title translates as "Pioneers of Japanese Development." He wrote that the original *Issei* settlers were true "pioneers of racial development [who] have endured poor living conditions, patiently fought exclusion and persecution day and night and still established the basis for social progress."[3] By this account the *Issei* attacked the wilderness in the same way as white Americans, becoming true pioneers who transformed barren landscape into an agricultural wonderland. This was the story of "successful" entrepreneurs who deserved respect for their accomplishments and their ability to work together to forge a common identity for the benefit of the entire Japanese community in America.

The most famous of these pioneer publications, the 1940 *Zaibei Nihonjin-shi* (The History of Japanese in America) asserted that Japanese in America were from the beginning upright citizens and colonists who had a strong sense of commitment to their status as representatives of the Japanese nation. It is here also that we find one of the strongest embellishments of Okei-san, the superhero wonder woman who chartered the course for future generations of Japanese who ventured to the United States.

OKEI-SAN'S NEW IDENTITY

Okei's story and elevated status only began to appear in the 1920s. Her tombstone at Gold Hill was known to a few nearby Japanese residents who knew nothing of her past but who assumed that Okei was one of the many Japanese peasant women who had found their way to California at some earlier point in time. A curious *Issei* newspaperman came to the site of the

Wakamatsu colony in the early 1920s and interviewed local white residents who told him of Okei's story. The reporter returned to San Francisco and detailed his findings to the Japanese community. He introduced Okei-san to them, stressing that she was not a mere peasant, but rather a pioneer who voluntarily immigrated to this foreign land and who had tragically died young. A while later, a Japanese language teacher, Masahei Kawamura, popularized Okei's life and created a legend. He exalted her as the ideal pioneer woman in many articles and books.[4]

Kawamura wrote that the significance of Okei's grave lay in its "spiritual effect that runs like an electric current through the hearts of those who stand before it."[5] He also suggested that the Japanese community should commemorate the inspiring story of this pure and brave young woman who had sacrificed her life for the cause of Japanese pioneer development of California.[6]

These Japanese historians in California had already embellished the stories of the male farmer pioneers as people of noble qualities who heroically tamed the land. It then became necessary to equate the immigrant women with the same noble characteristics as their husbands. There would be no mention of the many uneducated Japanese women some of whom worked as prostitutes. To counter the negative perception of early immigrant women, *Issei* historians introduced the famous legend of Okei-san, said to be the first Japanese female to die in America. "The romanticism of Okei's story, as well as her pure young virginal state and short life enhanced her heroism and cleanliness in stark contrast to the 'disgraceful' lives of ordinary common women."[7] The authors of *Zaibei Nihonjinshi* put Okei-san at the top of its list of Japanese hero pioneers. The purity of Okei-san in effect cleansed the other *Issei* women who followed in later years. Her sacrifices and early death permitted her to become a symbol of the highly sanctified view of Japanese women in America.

Eiichiro Azuma writes:

> Since male Issei were not posited as the inferior stock of *dekasegi* laborers, immigrant women had to match their husbands' qualities as pioneer settlers. To counter the negative perception of early immigrant women, many of whom came to the West Coast as prostitutes, Issei historians introduced the famous legend of Okei—claimed to be the first Japanese female in America. The romanticism of Okei's story, as well as her virginal state and short life, advanced her heroism and cleanliness.[8]

Fred Kochi, a fourth-generation Japanese American who acted as a spokesman for several groups with an interest in the colony, noted in 2007 that "Okei-san personifies the immigrant spirit. She is a popular folk hero here and in Japan,"[9] where a replica of her tombstone stands at a shrine in the modern city of Aizu-Wakamatsu.

The transformation of Okei-san from a forgotten dead Japanese teenager into a virtual saint drew attention to her grave. Ethnic Japanese began in their minds to monumentalize her gravesite as a key element in the pioneer story of Japanese in America. They cleared away all the brush around the grave and made the fading inscription legible by adding black ink. At the biannual convention of the Japanese American Citizens League in 1934, representatives voted to "beautify the grave of Miss Okei, the first Japanese woman pioneer." Setting up a special fund, they proclaimed, "Miss Okei has carved a niche in the memory of her contemporaries and her posterity. Her name is now tradition, an inspiration that has guided others to pioneer along the same lines."[10]

It did not take long for news of Okei's symbolic deification to reach Japan. A well-known literary scholar, Takeshi Kimura, is credited not only with the first full-scale hijacking of the Okei-san legend in Japan, but for being the first scholar to put her image to use in Japan in support of a program of Japanese expansion to mainland East Asia.

Kimura went to California and made an impromptu visit to Okei-san's grave at Gold Hill. After his return to Japan, in 1932 he published an article in a popular Sunday magazine about his visit and Okei-san's life. He reported that while interviewing area residents about Okei-san, he felt that "the bravery of the beautiful girl Okei, first woman to venture to California in 1870" inspired him so much that he was determined to learn more about her for a book project. Three years later Kimura published a novel, *Meiji Kensetsu: Erudorado no Okei* ("Building Meiji: Okei in Eldorado," 1935) where Okei was transformed into a forerunner not simply of Japanese emigration but of "Japanese imperialism."[11]

The novel is a work of pure fiction that takes place against the backdrop of the Meiji Restoration of 1868. The main characters are Fukuzawa Yukichi, the real-life strong proponent of Japan's westernization and founder of what is today one of Japan's foremost schools, Keio University; Okei-san; and Shijimi Heikuro, a totally fictional character who is placed as a student at Keio. When the imperial forces battle pro-Tokugawa forces in 1868 outside Tokyo and later in Aizu, Shijimi joins the imperial army, but is blinded by an exploding shell during the battle of Aizu. He is taken in by a family there and encounters Okei-san, who is a robust assassin for the Aizu clan. The blind Shijimi and Okei fall in love and a brief romance ensues, but Okei disappears by the time Shijimi regains his eyesight. They meet again a short time later in Yokohama, where Okei is about to depart for California with the Schnell party. She dies in California a couple of years later, while Shijimi goes on to promote Japanese nationalist causes in his homeland.[12]

Historian Eiichiro Azuma writes that several ideological messages are implicit in the fictional conversations between Shijimi and Okei-san after their meeting in Yokohama. This was written in 1935, shortly after Japan had seized Manchuria from China. Talk of Okei-san leading a group of Japanese pioneers to America really implied Japan's current policy of encouraging pioneers to move on to Manchuria in the mid-1930s to strengthen Japan's claim to the region. In the novel, Shijimi is amazed when Okei-san tells him that she and her fellow pioneers were off to America to establish a Japanese village on its frontier. "This young woman is heading for America!" he muttered for "even I, a student of Western studies have never dared to think of such a thing." Shijimi cautions Okei-san about the seemingly unrealistic nature of her task, pointing out that even now there were no remnants left of Japanese settlements made many generations ago in Southeast Asia. Okei's reply surprised Shijimi: "That's because our ancestors did not take hoes with them." Some, according to her, "took swords and conquered foreign places," and others "took abacuses in pursuit of profits only."

Okei-san continued,

> No way could they sink roots by such means. With hoes, they should have cultivated the land, developed rice fields, and grown vegetables—in other words—they should have engaged in agriculture. Then, I think the Japanese villages in Southeast Asia could have remained prosperous even today. . . . And farming takes more than male labor. Perhaps, warfare and commerce would only need men, but farming requires women to raise families. A Japanese settlement would thrive only if men farm to sink roots in the land and women produce descendants for them.[13]

Kimura, through this fabricated conversation between Shijimi and Okei-san, is linking the peaceful expansion of Japanese to the American West in 1869 to the contemporary Japanese colonization of Manchuria. Okei-san had spearheaded the original family-based agricultural expansion of Japan which had culminated in the emigration of over one hundred thousand Japanese by the 1920s. The alleged success of Japanese agriculturalists in California and elsewhere provided a clear example of what Kimura and other Japanese expansionists hope to achieve in Manchuria. Kimura has Okei-san advocating the emigration of tens of thousands of Japanese families to plant a permanent Japanese presence on the mainland.[14]

Kimura's 1935 novel became a major Japanese motion picture produced by the Toho Cinema Company titled "The Flower in the Storm" (*Arashi ni Saku Hana;* 1940). In the film, Okei-san and Shijimi return but are markedly different from the people they were in the original book. Okei-san is now a fierce female warrior and assassin from a samurai agricultural family. She fights valiantly to save her family farms and her Aizu homeland, but when it is lost she determines to lead another quest, the Japanese colonization of the American West. The film ends with Okei-san leading her party of hearty colonists to their rendezvous with destiny. There is no mention of Okei's early death or the failure of the Wakamatsu venture. Eiichiro Azuma writes:

> Without the insertion of her death and her colony's failure, the film immortalized Okei and the Wakamatsu colony, and through the absence of vital historical information it hinted at a direct causal linkage between her and Japanese development in the United States and other new Japans, including "Manchukuo." In "The Flower in the Storm," the past was not simply a historical crystal ball for a different present; in it, what was unfolding in Manchuria directly mirrored what had happened in America.[15]

Today the legendary mythical tale of Okei-san has waned both for Japanese Americans and for Japanese abroad, but we still hear stories of her heroism through various examples of modern fiction. Furthermore, her grave site remains the focus of visitations and pilgrimages. Her early death remains the most tangible element of the Wakamatsu colony site.

The late children's story writer, Joan Barton Barsotti (1939–2010) wrote a 1996 novel for young adults, *Okei-san: A Girl's Journey, Japan to California, 1868–1871*. Barsotti's fictional novel is the most widely read story of Okei's life even though much of the story took place only in the author's imagination. Nevertheless, Barsotti did a lot of research on Okei-san's life and wrote a brief essay describing her vision of the Japanese woman's life. I incorporate her essay here to give a more modern interpretation of Okei-san's life:

> Okei was 17 years old when she came to America in 1869 and only 19 when she died in 1871. I had stated repeatedly that I would never write a chapter book and I would never write a story with an unhappy ending! I am a picture book author and I enjoy writing cheerful stories for elementary school-age children. But, this is a local story, a true story about a girl who came to this country, probably not by choice, who worked very hard to do her best, and by so doing would honor her parents. She was a pioneer in every sense of the word. In 1868 Japan was embroiled in a civil war. Okei's hometown was destroyed, her family's whereabouts unknown. She came to California with a group of gardeners and samurai to start a tea and silk colony. The leader of the group, John Henry Schnell, was an honorary samurai. His wife Jou was the daughter of a samurai, and Okei was the nanny for the Schnell children. After two fairly successful years, the colony began to fail. Schnell went back to Japan promising to return with more supplies. He took his wife and two daughters, but left everyone else behind, including the nanny.
>
> This is my interpretation of Okei's story. I liked her very much. She was never able to overcome her homesickness, but she tried. She did not think she was courageous, but she was steadfast and loving. The neighbor, Louisa Veerkamp, loved her like a daughter. Matsu, the samurai, cared enough to have a tombstone made for her. She was just "Okei" when she came to America, but when Henry Veerkamp was interviewed many years later, he referred to her as "Okei-san" with the honorific title. For many years people have come to visit the gravesite, often from Japan. The gravesite is small; sits by itself atop a small hill overlooking the Gold Trail School, and beyond that, thousands of

miles away, Japan. Okei was never forgotten. Could it be that she was somebody special, after all? I think so.[16]

There are several factual errors here. Okei-san probably came to California during the summer of 1870 in the company of farmworkers and carpenters, not gardeners and samurai. And Okei-san's grave site was largely forgotten for nearly fifty years after her death, until it was rediscovered by *Issei* and *Nisei* historians who sought out the Wakamatsu colony and the young teenage girl who died there. Nevertheless, Barsotti's statement presents us with a more modern view of her young Japanese heroine, and her grave remains the centerpiece of the Wakamatsu colony site.

During one of my several visits to Okei's gravesite, I encountered three young Japanese, two men and a woman, leaving as I arrived. I asked in Japanese why they were there. The young woman replied, "She is a symbol of Japanese in America. She became homesick and longed to return home, but her call to duty obliged her to stay. We honor her commitment to her duty and to her love for her family in Japan." A Wakamatsu Farm docent told me that she once encountered a Japanese visitor who thanked her for taking such good care of Okei-san. Clearly Okei the symbol continues to have an important place in the hearts of many Japanese and helps to make the Wakamatsu Farm an important pilgrimage site for many Japanese Americans who venture there every year.

NOTES

1. Quoted in Eiichiro Azuma, *Between Two Empires: Race, History, and Transnationalism in Japanese America* (New York: Oxford University Press, 2005), 89–90.
2. Azuma, *Between Two Empires*, 89–90.
3. Quoted in Azuma, *Between Two Empires*, 91.
4. Azuma, *Between Two Empires*, 102–3.
5. Quoted in Azuma, 103.
6. Gordon Chang et al, *Before Internment: Essays in Prewar Japanese-American History* (Stanford: Stanford University Press, 2006), 81.
7. Azuma, *Between Two Empires*, 102.
8. Azuma, *Between Two Empires*, 102.
9. *Los Angeles Times*, June 10, 2007.
10. Quoted in Azuma, *Between Two Empires*, 104.
11. Eiichiro Azuma, "'Pioneers of Overseas Japanese Development': Japanese American History and the Making of Expansionist Orthodoxy in Imperial Japan," *Journal of Asian Studies* 67, no. 4 (2008): 1202.
12. Azuma, *JAS*, 1201.
13. Azuma, *JAS*, 1203.
14. Azuma, *JAS*, 1204.
15. Azuma, *JAS*, 1205.
16. http://www.abebooks.it/servlet/BookDetailsPL?bi=21752575603&searchurl=tn%3Dokei%2Bsan%2Bgirls%2Bjourney%2Bjapan%26sortby%3D17 (accessed October 1, 2017).

Chapter Eight

Wakamatsu as a Pilgrimage Site

A pilgrimage is a journey or search for a place that carries sentimental, moral, or spiritual significance for the person making the journey. Many social or national groups have one or more places that symbolize their origins. When traveling in Turkey several years ago, I met a stream of Australian tourists making the long journey to the Turkish region of the Gallipoli Peninsula. They told me that they were on a pilgrimage to the site of the great World War I battle between British and allied forces and the Turkish army, then fighting with Germany. Thousands of Australian troops supporting the British died there, marking one of the first times that a truly Australian army had tasted war. Several of these Australians told me that they were making this pilgrimage because in their opinion Gallipoli was the time and place where the modern nation of Australia was truly born.

The United States has several pilgrimage sites. There are, of course, Plymouth Rock in Massachusetts and Jamestown and Williamsburg in Virginia, as well as the bridge at Concord, Massachusetts, and Independence Hall in Philadelphia. Hundreds of thousands of Americans visit these sites every year.

Every culture has its creation or Genesis story, and Japanese Americans are no exception. Japanese love festivals, and many temples and shrines in Japan hold annual fests that bring communities together while celebrating their origins. Japanese Americans have continued this tradition often attending occasional festivals at the site of the Wakamatsu colony, where they can participate in a memorial Buddhist ceremony at the grave of Okei-san, look for their own roots, and sing and dance in a very traditional Japanese manner.

Although the Wakamatsu colony had little direct relevance to the massive diaspora of Japanese to North America that started a generation later, many ethnic Japanese today make the journey to the Wakamatsu Farm site and to

Okei-san's grave because it serves as a symbolic representation of finding their roots. Japanese Americans can honor the brave little colony which launched the Japanese experience in America and where Okei-san became a symbol serving the expansion of Japanese civilization to a new world.

John Van Sant writes:

> While the colonists from Aizu had minimal direct influence on the course of relations between the United States and Japan, their departure from Japan as refugees, their intention to settle permanently in the United States, and their establishment of an agricultural colony would soon be imitated by thousands of Japanese immigrants.[1]

The Wakamatsu farmland and the grave of Okei Ito have indeed become important pilgrimage spots for many Japanese Americans. Fred Kochi, a spokesman in the Japanese American community with a deep interest in the history and legacy of the Wakamatsu colony, told a reporter for the *Los Angeles Times* in 2007 that "To the Japanese, Okei-san personifies the immigrant spirit. She is a popular folk hero here and in Japan."[2]

The late Henty Taketa, a well-respected attorney, historian, and Sacramento Japanese American community leader, recounted how the Wakamatsu colony "passed into oblivion and its existence was forgotten until after World War I." At that time, according to Taketa, some community leaders heard vague rumors that a Japanese girl had died in northern California during the Gold Rush era. An interested group of Sacramentans researched these rumors and finally made their way to Coloma and Gold Hill in 1924. There they encountered Henry Veerkamp, then seventy-five, who had been a teenager when the Wakamatsu Japanese arrived and when Sakurai and Okei-san came to live with his family after John Henry Schnell, his wife and children, as well as the other Japanese workers had all left. Veerkamp led these curious visitors to the farmhouse that had served as the nerve center of the colony and to the summit of the small hill where Okei's grave is located. "Thus," Taketa wrote, "the Wakamatsu Tea and Silk Farm was rediscovered."[3]

Veerkamp, who was one year older than Okei-san, remembered her well and gladly passed on these memories to the very appreciative group from Sacramento. Since that visit and the discovery of the grave, Taketa wrote, "Okei has been spiritually enshrined in the hearts of many Japanese who, like Okei, came to the new world in their youth with not more than hopes and dreams but, unlike Okei, through sweat and toil saw their dreams come true."[4]

Okei-san was buried on the knoll of a small hill near the farmhouse where it is said that she would watch the setting sun and gaze in the direction of her distant homeland in Aizu-Wakamatsu. Okei's life story eventually made its way from these Japanese Americans to her hometown, and so moved city residents that they constructed a memorial, dedicated in 1957 to Okei-san and the other Wakamatsu Colony pioneers. The memorial park, which overlooks the city of Aizu-Wakamatsu, includes a replica of Okei-san's gravestone at Gold Hill.

Professor Wayne Maeda, who taught Asian American Studies at Sacrament State University for four decades before his death in 2013, wrote that the site of the Wakamatsu Colony is important "because it represents the adventurous spirit of the Issei generation. . . . To risk all in a new and unknown land to seek their dreams. . . . Dreams of riches, dreams of a new place, dreams of starting anew. . . . [It also] represents the dreams that many other who followed later brought with them."[5]

Maeda stressed that the importance of the Wakamatsu settlement goes far beyond the fact that it was the first sizable Japanese settlement in this country. The birth of the Schnell family's second daughter Mary at Gold Hill marked the first multiracial Nisei born on the mainland. Maeda concluded, "Okei-san was the first Issei woman to die in America." The marriage of another colonist, Kuninosuke Masumizu, with an African-American woman was the first interracial marriage on American soil. Maeda concluded, "I think they were in general a metaphor for those who followed in greater numbers beginning in the late 1880s."[6]

THE IMPORTANCE OF EVENTS

Celebrations are a very important pastime in Japanese culture because they bring communities together to celebrate their past and to renew ties for the present and future. Occasional festivals at the site of the Wakamatsu colony serve this same function. The 2017 pilgrimage sponsored by the San Francisco-based Nichi Bei Foundation is a case in point.

Early in 2017 Nichi Bei Foundation announced that it was going to sponsor a major pilgrimage at the Wakamatsu Colony site on October 7, 2017. The goal of the exercise was to better acquaint interested persons, especially Japanese Americans, with the history of the Wakamatsu Colony. This history is the key to understanding the growth of the Japanese American community in North America and to develop a greater appreciation of the struggles of the Issei generation during the latter half of the nineteenth century. A related goal is to help Japanese Americans find their roots and to provide others with a greater appreciation of the contributions that Japanese Americans have made to the betterment of American society.

The Nichi Bei Foundation (literally translated as the Japan U.S. Foundation) is an educational and charitable nonprofit organization whose goal is to keep the Japanese American community informed, connected, and empowered through its newspaper, the *Nichi Bei Weekly,* as well as through a variety of educational programs. It "strives to be the glue that holds the community together, helping to preserve Japanese culture while shedding light on community issues and documenting the community's history for generations to come."

The roots of the Nichi Bei Foundation go back to 1899, when a Japanese newspaper seller, Kyutaro Abiko, founded a daily newspaper, the *Nichibei Shinbun,* for the Japanese American community. The newspaper thrived through the prewar period, drawing a circulation of twenty-five thousand during the 1920s. World War II brought a termination of the newspaper, but a successor, the *Nich Bei Times,* emerged in 1946. Publication continued through 2009, when declining circulation and revenues forced its termination. Today the nucleus of what was the Nichi Bei newspaper is the Nichi Bei Foundation and its online publication, the *Nichi Bei Weekly.*

California historian Art Hansen made the following appraisal of the Foundation and its work:

> The work done by the (Nichi Bei) Foundation, not only through its stalwart newspaper, but also through the enlightened and dedicated sponsorship of a dizzying array of activities, renders it arguably the extant Nikkei institution that makes the single greatest contribution to the maintenance and enrichment of the history, society, and culture of the Japanese American community.[7]

The fact that the Wakamatsu Colony site has become a key pilgrimage destination is clear in the notice that the Nichi Bei Foundation made for its October 7, 2017, pilgrimage there:

> Join us for an inaugural biennial pilgrimage to the site of the first large settlement of Japanese in America. A national and state historic landmark, the Wakamatsu Tea and Silk Colony was established June 8, 1869 as the first Japanese colony in the U.S. It is also the birthplace of the first Japanese American, and the gravesite of the first Japanese woman buried in the U.S., Okei Ito.
>
> This year's pilgrimage is a rare opportunity to learn about the storied history of this colony led by John Schnell and former samurai from Aizu-Wakamatsu, present-day Fukushima Prefecture, Japan.
>
> Participants can trace their own roots through family history consultations with volunteers from the California Genealogical Society.[8]

The Nichi Bei Foundation arranged a program for this recent festival which included the following:

- **Wakamatsu Tea and Silk Colony Farm tours and exhibits**, including the Okei Ito gravesite and Graner House
- **Gene Gibson, great-great grandson of Kuninosuke Masumizu**, a former *samurai* and Wakamatsu Colony settler

- Talk on the Japanese immigrant experience by **SF State University Asian American Studies Professor Christen Sasaki, Ph.D.**
- **FREE Family History Consultations** with volunteers from the California Genealogical Society
- Preview of Wakamatsu Colony Farm renovation and **WakaFest150**
- Blessing by **Rev. Ronald Kobata,** Buddhist Church of San Francisco
- *Taiko* drum performance by **Placer Ume Taiko**
- **Bento lunch** included in fees
- Wakamatsu Colony-related books for sale
- Craft activity

This pilgrimage was a marked success. There were about 200 guests, including about 150 from the Bay area. One of the many events, a graveside Buddhist prayer service in honor of Okei-san, was well attended and "very moving" according to some of the participants.

The October 2017 event is one in a long series of similar events. A May 2012 festival at the Wakamatsu Colony was constructed along the same lines. It included speeches by notables including Professor Maeda; a Buddhist ceremony conducted by a Japanese Buddhist priest at the grave site of Okei-san; Japanese dances performed by a group of elderly Japanese American women; an enthusiastic *taiko* drum performance; and several other events. A busload of Japanese tourists arrived in time to partake in the ceremonies.

A major celebration is planned for June 2019 to commemorate the 150th anniversary of the founding of the Wakamatsu colony, but in the meantime both individuals and groups of ethnic Japanese and others continue to visit the site and pay their respects at the grave of Okei-san.

NOTES

1. John E. Van Sant, *Pacific Pioneers: Japanese Journeys to America and Hawaii, 1850–80* (Urbana and Chicago: University of Illinois Press, 2000), 130.
2. *Los Angeles Times*, June 10, 2007.
3. Kenji G. Takuma, "Where It All Began: Preserving the First Settlement of Japanese Americans," *Nichi Bei Times*, April 26, 2007.
4. Takuma, "Where It All Began."
5. Takuma, "Where It All Began."
6. Takuma, "Where It All Began."
7. http://www.nichibei.org/about/nichibeifoundation/ (accessed September 10, 2017).
8. http://www.nichibei.org/wakamatsu-pilgrimage/ (accessed September 10, 2017).

Chapter Nine

What Happened to the Wakamatsu Colonists?

Since the 1850s, the United States and Japan have developed an intensely close relationship that can be characterized as a kind of marriage between a very unlikely couple. The United States and Japan knew very little about each other before 1850, but it was the American navy under the leadership of Commodore Matthew Perry that first "opened" Japan in 1853 and 1854 and signed the first commercial treaty with the Tokugawa Shogunate in 1858. Many of the foreign teachers who came to Japan in the 1870s and 1880s were American, and President Theodore Roosevelt was Japan's greatest champion during the Russo-Japanese War of 1904–1905. The relationship deteriorated in the early twentieth century to such an extent that the two nations became embroiled in a ruinous war after the infamous 1941 attack on Pearl Harbor. However, the United States played a dominant and constructive role during the allied occupation of Japan (1945–1952) and has enjoyed a close political, military, business, and cultural relationship ever since.

The Japanese who arrived in Gold Hill, California, in 1869 and 1870 came to the United States as refugees from a bitter civil war that had destroyed their homes and livelihoods in Aizu. Unlike the other tiny handful of Japanese living in the United States at that time, who were mainly students in American high schools and colleges on the East coast, they came to the United States hoping to remain as permanent residents. Their reception by Americans was generally positive. Newspaper reports acclaimed them as a hardworking model minority who posed no threats to white Americans and were far more desirable than the much-despised Chinese. The agricultural goods that they brought with them and their intense work on their farm after their arrival indicated that their stay was permanent and that, if successful, other refugees from Japan would soon join them from Aizu.

Sadly, the Aizu Japanese were too few in number and knew little about their new environment. Ironically, the 1870 U.S. census indicates only fifty-five Japanese in the United States, twenty-two of them (40 percent) at Wakamatsu Farm. War had devastated their Aizu domain, leaving them with little or no money. They had to start their new lives without the necessary financial backing. Their German-born patron, John Henry Schnell, was one of the first people in Japan who conceived of the idea of Japanese refugees migrating to the United States. He had the foresight to realize that these Japanese refugees had to have a profitable livelihood if they were to remain in the United States on a permanent basis.

The Wakamatsu colony was an advance party of farmers, other workmen, and some families, who came to determine whether California and the United States could serve as a place where they could start their lives over. They were true pioneers, but they, led by John Henry Schnell, came too early and too unprepared to make a go of it on their own. Nevertheless, the examples they set became a true harbinger for future immigrants who came a generation later.

WHAT HAPPENED TO THE JAPANESE COLONISTS?

The Wakamatsu Tea and Silk Farm Colony came to a sad end when the Schnell family waved good-bye to the remaining inhabitants of the farm and disappeared into oblivion in early June 1871. By then, however, most of the workers had left, and we have few clues as to their fate. Did they all return to Japan? Did some stay in California and work at other jobs? Sadly, we know something about only five of the workers.

John Van Sant provides an overview of the dispersal of the workers:

> With the demise of the colony, the Japanese dispersed to nearby areas. Some went to San Francisco and sought the help of Charles Brooks, Japan's consul general. Existing records of the Fukuinkai (Gospel Society) indicate that two or three people from the disbanded Wakamatsu Colony were among this organization's first members. A few are believed to have made their way back to Japan and Aizu by way of the Pacific Mail steamships departing from San Francisco. If so, their return was apparently kept quiet because they were still considered enemies of the Meiji government.[1]

OKEI-SAN AND MATSUNOSUKE SAKURAI

When the Schnell family left by June 1871, they left behind their daughter's Japanese nanny, Okei Ito, as well as one of the male workers, Matsunosuke Sakurai, who some believe had been a samurai before the fall of the Aizu domain. By then, all of the other Japanese workers had left the colony in search of work elsewhere. The Veerkamp family took them both in and seemingly welcomed them as members of their own family.

Matsunosuke Sakurai was the one and only member of the Wakamatsu Colony who never left the area. He lived with the Veerkamp family and worked for them as a gardener, truck farmer, and all-around handyman. He served the Veerkamp family until his death on February 23, 1901, and is buried in the cemetery in Coloma. The American River Conservancy believes it has found the unmarked grave of Matsunosuke in the Coloma cemetery and recently placed a small gravestone at that spot.

ARC volunteer Herb Tanimoto writes:

> Matsu began his next life as a foreman in the Veerkamp family's fruit and produce business. He was a distribution manager responsible for the western part of California to San Francisco, a task he performed with his usual fortitude. In addition, Veerkamp lore says that he managed to find time to become a wonderful gardener around the farmhouse. This was to be his life for 30 years.
>
> Veerkamp family members tended to his needs when he became ill. After his death in 1901, a respectful service and burial at the Coloma Cemetery was arranged. A simple marker was placed on a sturdy oak tree by his grave. Unfortunately, the tree fell down and the location became lost in the intervening years. The samurai who had made sure that Okei's resting place was not forgotten would himself become forgotten.[2]

Interestingly, the 1880 manuscript census of El Dorado County shows Sakurai living with one other Japanese man in nearby Coloma, at least one of whom may have been one of the original colonists.[3]

OTHER JAPANESE SURVIVORS

One of the reasons that the Wakamatsu Tea and Silk Farm Colony is compared to some of the early English settlements in North America is that while they were "first," they did not survive for long. Another point is that when the Colony ceased operations by the spring and early summer of 1871, most of the Japanese workers had left, perhaps to other jobs or to return to Japan. There is no evidence that any of the workers beyond the four discussed here plus Okei-san stayed much longer in California, but when or if they ever returned to Japan will probably remain a mystery. We are lucky that in recent years the fate of Ofuji Matsugoro and Sakichi Yanagisawa became known, and maybe some of the others will resurface. One never knows.

The pioneer colonists may or may not have had permission to depart from Japan for California in 1869 and 1870, but if any of them returned in the 1870s, they probably did so quietly without much fanfare so as not to garner much attention. Unfortunately we do not have the travel rosters of many ships during this period to determine when or if any of these colonists returned to Japan. We may never know their true identities, where they came from, and what they did after they left Gold Hill.

THE LIVES OF OFUJI MATSUGORO AND SAKICHI YANAGISAWA [4]

Sometimes, lucky researchers can stumble upon apparently lost aspects of history by sheer accident. According to the American River Conservancy, such was the case in 2014 when Naori Shiraishi, a then sixteen-year-old high school student in Tokyo, made an amazing discovery. Japanese high school students are routinely assigned homework over their brief summer vacations. Naori's project was to research her family roots. Through her own research and discussions with one of her great uncles, she discovered that Ofuji Matsugoro, her fourth paternal great-grandfather, had been a member of the Wakamatsu Tea and Silk Colony.

Matsugoro (c. 1822–1890) was about forty-five years old when he traveled to California with the Wakamatsu Colony in 1869. With him came his wife and their baby daughter Sakuko. ARC wonders whether Sakuko was born in Japan or in California. If born in California, she would have been only the second baby of Japanese descent born on American soil—John Henry Schnell's daughter Mary, born in early spring of 1870 in Coloma, might well have been the first.[5] Matsugoro worked at the Wakamatsu Colony as a carpenter. After the collapse of the Colony in the summer of 1871, he and his fellow colonist Kuninosuke Masuzumi used their skills as carpenters to take part in the building of the nearby Coloma Hotel in the town of Coloma.

His whereabouts soon after leaving Coloma are unclear. We know that he and another recently discovered colonist, Sakichi Yanagisawa, were studying viticulture in the Fresno area of California for a full year, having been sent there by the Japanese government in 1875. It is well known that Matsugoro and Yanagisawa returned to Japan in 1876 with his family and settled with them in Yamanashi Prefecture in central Japan southwest of Tokyo. He became a leading pioneer in the Japanese fruit-processing industry, performing experimentation on canning peaches and tomatoes in Tokyo. By 1877, he directed the introduction of fermenting equipment for wine in the Prefectural Institute for Wine and later became the chief engineer in the winery in Yamanashi.

What we don't know is whether Matsugoro returned to Japan and then came back to California in 1875 or if he was in California between 1871 and 1875. Matsugoro died in 1890 at approximately sixty-eight years of age.

Katazina Joanna Cwiertka in her 2015 book *Modern Japanese Cuisine: Food, Power and National Identity,* writes:

> Yanagisawa Sakichi and Ōfuji Matsugorō, both returnees from a study trip in the United States, were the first to can peaches and tomatoes [in Japan]. Their canning tests were conducted at the Interior Ministry's Laboratory for the Promotion of Agriculture in Shinjuku, Tokyo. The laboratory not only worked on the mastering of the canning process itself, but also put effort in canning machinery that the Japanese bureaucrats had purchased in Europe and the United States.[6]

KUNINOSUKE MASUMIZU

The best source for information about Wakamatsu colonist Kuninosuke Masumizu (c. 1849–1915) is John Van Sant in his book *Pacific Pioneers.*[7] He writes that Masumizu

> was a twenty-year-old carpenter when he arrived at Gold Hill with the second group from Aizu in the fall of 1869. After the breakup of the colony, he worked as miner and farmer in Coloma. In 1877, he married Carrie Wilson, a woman of black and American Indian heritage. They had three children who survived infancy and lived near James Marshall's cabin on a hillside overlooking the American River. According to their granddaughter, the family had a hard time making a living in Coloma. The family moved to Sacramento sometime after 1880, where Masumizu continued to work as a farmer and a miner, in addition to stints as a cook, a barber and a fisherman. His grandson recalled that Masumizu was "quite a fisherman. I used to go to the river and fish with him." He had one major weakness, however. "He was a gambler, and my grandmother didn't like it," his granddaughter Juanita Wong told an interviewer. Masumizu seemed to be something of a loner, and around 1910 he left his family in Sacramento and drifted north to Colusa, where he died in 1915 at the age of sixty-six.

Masumizu is said to have spoken four languages and at times acted as an interpreter for courts in Sacramento.

According to his grandson George Elebeck, Masumizu was not subjected to racial discrimination during his lifetime, perhaps because he did not look Japanese. "You couldn't very well tell my grandfather was Japanese until you looked close at him or talked to him. He looked more like an Indian," Elebeck recalled. However, after the attack on Pearl Harbor in December 1941, eighty-five-year-old Carrie Masumizu, her children, and her grandchildren—who considered themselves African American—were all interrogated by the FBI to determine if they were enemy aliens because Masumizu, dead for more than twenty-six years, was Japanese.

We know nothing more about the other twenty or so workers who came from Japan. The list of names on the 1870 census sheet can tell us something about the ages and occupations of the workers, but because of the intense language barrier, the names were all garbled. We should even be a bit wary of the ages listed, because the traditional Japanese way of counting age is different from that of the West. For example, a Japanese born on Christmas Day in 1849 would be considered two years old on New Year's Day, 1850. Another factor is that it was quite rare for commoners in Japan to have last names. Taking a last name was a practice adopted at the outset of the Meiji era, thus making it hard for historians today to track their movements.

Today there is renewed interest in the fate of the Wakamatsu pioneers. The hope is that future researchers both in Japan and the United States will research and publish more about these intrepid people who so bravely tried to find a new life in America.

NOTES

1. John E. Van Sant, *Pacific Pioneers: Japanese Journeys to America and Hawaii, 1850–80* (Urbana and Chicago: University of Illinois Press, 2000), 128.

2. Herb Tanimoto, "Honoring Matsunosuke Sakurai," *Wakamatsu Farm News*, Spring 2017, 6.

3. We assume that this is Matsu, but his name is listed as Matz Suguri.

4. This section is based on an article, "Ofuji Matsugoro, Wakamatsu Colonist" by Wendy Guglieri in the January 2016 issue of the *Newsletter of the American River Conservancy*, 7.

5. According to the July 1, 1870, U.S. Census, Mary was two months old.

6. Katazina Joanna Cwiertka, *Modern Japanese Cuisine: Food, Power and National Identity* (New York: Reaktion Books, 2015), 62.

7. Van Sant, *Pacific Pioneers*, 128.

Afterword

Conserving Wakamatsu Farm — American River Conservancy

Melissa Lobach

Melissa Lobach is the campaign and communication manager for the American River Conservancy, which owns the 272-acre farmland settled by the Wakamatsu Colonists, including Okei's grave site. She helps the conservancy operate the farm by writing grants, planning tours and events, overseeing projects and programs, coordinating volunteers, and communicating with the public. Melissa is a certified interpretive guide, California naturalist, and a seasonal park aide for California State Parks. She has been a Wakamatsu Farm docent since 2011.

Within three miles of the town called Coloma where California gold was first discovered, the beginning of Japanese-American culture can still be found. It began when the first Japanese pioneers in America arrived at a Gold Hill site to establish their tea and silk farm on June 8, 1869. One hundred years later marked the Japanese American centennial, and the site of the *Wakamatsu Tea and Silk Farm Colony* was commemorated with the unveiling of California Registered Historical Landmark No. 815. The monument is still located in the parking lot of Gold Trail School within eyesight of Okei-san's grave.

During the 1969 landmark ceremony, then Governor Ronald Reagan arrived by helicopter and spoke to a small audience. Fifty years later, members of that same crowd tell that story when they are visiting or volunteering at the Farm. When the timing is right, they and the general public might also meet the descendants of Wakamatsu colonists or other historical residents of the Farm. Such rare and real "living history" is now made possible by the efforts of the American River Conservancy (ARC). This is the story of how ARC literally stepped up to "save the Farm" and became the owner and operator of the place now called Wakamatsu Farm.

To begin, some background about the Conservancy and its range. ARC has operated primarily as a nonprofit land trust since 1989 within the Western slope of California's central Sierra Nevada mountain range. Based in Coloma, ARC's mission is to "serve our communities by ensuring healthy ecosystems within the upper American River and upper Cosumnes River watersheds through land conservation, stewardship, and education." At the time of this publication, ARC has purchased and protected over twenty-five thousand acres of land within these critical watersheds, which provide fresh water to the Sacramento region and beyond.

After ARC acquires a property, it restores and stewards the land to minimize any unhealthy human footprints. ARC welcomes more healthy human footprints by building scenic trails on its most stunning properties. ARC has given more than half of its acquired lands back to the public via donations to government land management agencies, such as the U.S. Forest Service and Bureau of Land Management. In this way, ARC has created over thirty miles of beautiful public recreational trails mainly along the American River and within easy driving distance of the Sacramento metropolitan area.

ARC's protected lands encompass wild and scenic rivers, ancient forests, endangered species, and vital habitats from the wilderness near South Lake Tahoe to the suburbs near the city of Folsom. As a defender of public lands from ravages of rapid residential development, ARC's supporters are like-minded conservationists. Added to ARC's stock of environmental activists, citizen scientists, educators, land stewards, volunteers, hikers, riders, and all around nature-lovers, are now the culture keepers of Japanese American heritage and frequent visitors from Japan. The results of ARC's hard work draws this eclectic blend of people to the rural, largely agricultural community of El Dorado County, which includes the tourist-friendly farms of Apple Hill.

El Dorado County contains approximately one million acres of national forest land, but it is probably most appreciated for its productive small farms, quaint fruit orchards, expanding vineyards and wineries, and world-class white-water river rafting. A diverse recreational area, most of the County includes the picturesque backdrop of native oak woodlands or sweeping vistas of subalpine forests. In the foothills, huge tracts of California dream homes are also under construction. Given all the land has to offer, no small wonder the County remains locked in competition for its precious, clean water. Seemingly abundant, high-quality water keeps El Dorado County growing. Readers of this work may also recall the lack of good water assured the Japanese Colony's demise. Water has its own history lessons.

Located in the American River watershed, Wakamatsu Farm has ample water during normal rainfall years. The 272-acre property includes three ponds and the headwaters of Granite and Shingle Creeks. All types of Sierra foothill habitats are found at the Farm, including woodland, wetland, riparian, grassland habitats, and even soils of statewide importance. The majority of the Farm is undeveloped, thus ideal for environmental study. The ponds and riparian areas support healthy populations of western pond turtle, Sierran tree frog, and over twenty species of resident and migratory waterfowl. Large portions of the property are covered in blue oak and interior live oak woodlands with an array of low elevation seasonal wetlands along with fields of annual grasses and native wildflowers. Conserving the land's natural resources is one of ARC's primary goals for the property, although preserving its cultural history was ARC's main reason for acquiring Wakamatsu Farm.

The cultural assets of the property long predate the Wakamatsu Colony, as people have been intricately connected to the land long before recorded time. The artifacts of two farming centuries show up around the property, common reminders of the Graner and Veerkamp families, much of it rusting, weathered, and hazardous. Ages before the farmers lived countless generations of native Californians, the Nisenan people, who prospered throughout the region for millennia before the gold rush migration devastated their populations. At times, digging in the soil or clearing brush at the Farm yields more than expected, which is not so unusual given the area. Other ARC properties have similar features, including ramshackle structures and ancient bedrock mortars near riverbanks.

In many ways, Wakamatsu Farm is like the rest of ARC's land holdings. But what makes the property different and most worthy of conservation is its Japanese history. Wakamatsu Farm is the site of the first Japanese Colony in America settled by immigrants who intended to stay. It is the birthplace of the first Japanese child documented in America. It contains the grave of the first Japanese woman and immigrant who died and was buried on American soil. This trifecta story of "firsts" includes a beginning, middle, and end. The Farm's Japanese history is outstanding, unparalleled in America, and distinct in all the world.

The site of so many "firsts" for Japanese Americans is also the site of several "firsts" for ARC. Wakamatsu Farm is the Conservancy's first cultural landmark property. It is ARC's first working farm and residential address where people permanently live. Wakamatsu Farm is also how many people first encounter ARC's work of preserving rivers and lands for life. The beauty, location, and history of the Farm are powerful public lures. Wakamatsu Farm represents the most precious resources El Dorado County offers and the Conservancy strives to protect for posterity. For all these reasons, ARC entered the Wakamatsu Farm picture decades ago.

ARC's collaboration to purchase and protect Wakamatsu Farm began in the mid-1990s when Gene Itogawa of the Sacramento Japanese American Citizens League and ARC's longtime Executive Director, Alan Ehrgott, agreed to work together to monitor the ownership of the Farm. Admirers of the land and its fascinating history, they long anticipated the opportunity when the property might become available for sale. The opportunity came in 2007 when the Veerkamp family approached ARC with an offer to sell the Farm at fair-market value. ARC commissioned the appraisal, and a purchase agreement was struck to acquire the property for its appraised value of $3,200,000. This was the value of the land subdivided as "ranchettes," as it would have gone to market for sale. No appraised value was allocated to any of the Farm buildings, which were long vacated and literally falling apart at the seams.

In the difficult financial years of 2008 through 2010, $1.9 million in purchase funding was raised. ARC closed escrow and bought the 272-acre property in October 2010 with $1.3 million remaining in mortgage loans. Debt of this scale was unusual for ARC. Substantial funding was promised from both the California State Parks and a benefactor in Fukushima Prefecture, Japan. But the forces of nature and man can be equally unpredictable and unfortunate. An economic downturn in America and a devastating tsunami in Japan left ARC in debt for a portion of the outstanding loan with little to no backup options. To date, ARC manages the Farm debt as a monthly mortgage payment. For this reason, one of ARC's most pressing goals is to resolve the debt and make the Farm entirely self-sustaining. Attracting more funders, supporters, and visitors remains a Farm priority.

Meanwhile, much has improved around the Farm. ARC's partnership secured the placement of the Farm on the National Register of Historic Places at a level of national significance, which aids the ongoing quest for funding. The Conservancy secured a $483,000 grant from the California Cultural and Historical Endowment to complete the structural stabilization of the 1850s farmhouse that was once home for the Wakamatsu colonists. Later, $200,000 in private donations and ARC general funds were used to restore the two resident homes, dairy, large barn, and sales barn. ARC also raised an additional $100,000 to develop an event center in and around the farmhouse. For the first time in history, the farmhouse has central heating and air. A new commercial kitchen in the farmhouse will be instrumental in future fundraising by supporting farm dinners and other charitable events for the Conservancy and community.

Wakamatsu Farm is also a working farm again. The Conservancy leases acreage to organic farming operations to help their businesses seed, grow, and thrive. Starting a new farm is brutally difficult in the best of circumstances, so ARC essentially subsidizes resident farmers by offering generous lease terms, including acreage, equipment, and housing. Currently, two privately owned farming operations are living and working on the land while supplying the community with sought-after organic produce, eggs, milk, and meat. In turn, these farms provide a small yearly income to help maintain Farm infrastructure and marginally pay down the mortgage.

ARC has always welcomed farming ideas that are rewarding to the land, farmers, and the Conservancy. It is fitting that the site of the first Japanese tea and silk farm in America will one day offer its own specialty tea label. A traditional Japanese teahouse on the Farm seems inevitable. Perhaps Japanese farmers will return to Wakamatsu Farm, maybe even farmers from Japan's Fukushima Prefecture who lost their livelihood after the tragic tsunami. Only new investors and funders will turn these possibilities into realities.

Additionally on the grounds, ARC's first crowdsourcing campaign secured the funds to service and stabilize the Japanese Elm tree (*Zelkova serrata*). Called a *keyaki*, in Japanese, the beloved tree is the only living remnant planted by the colonists. The massive Elm was also added to the California Big Tree Registry. The tree is greatly valued for its shapely beauty and shade over the farmhouse and adjoining garden. Onsite, ARC also maintains a native plant nursery for demonstration purposes and restoration projects. Underway is a grove of *sakura* (cherry blossom trees) for the beloved *hanami* (flower viewing) in years to come. Additionally, the Farm contains a fruit tree orchard and "giving garden" that pays its volunteers in food while contributing hundreds of pounds of fresh organic vegetables to local shelters and food banks each year.

When it comes to volunteers, ARC attracts around five hundred yearly who donate at least seven thousand hours each year. Much of their volunteer time is spent at Wakamatsu Farm where nothing humanly possible happens without their hard work. Farm volunteers are the everyday heroes who cheerfully help guests, plant trees, mow fields, pound nails, pull weeds, run machines, sweep floors, fix things, sing, dance, play, and tell the history and daily story of the Farm to everyone in earshot. Regular Farm volunteers enjoy a special camaraderie. They also enjoy the Farm more than anyone else because they are most often at the Farm.

The Conservancy is always seeking new volunteers to invigorate the Farm with their able and experienced hands and minds. Volunteer docents uncover fascinating new discoveries each year as they continuously conduct new research into the Farm and its historical residents. Volunteers also lead many yearly public and private events and tours, along with outreach and education programs. Each year, more school field trips, day camp trips, and overnight campouts happen at Wakamatsu Farm where children learn about agriculture, science, and nature while playing outside. Outdoor discovery in a natural playground is a luxury not every kid has these days.

To further the educational and outreach goals at the Farm, the funding and construction of an outdoor classroom near the main parking lot began in 2018. An outdoor classroom at the Farm is direly needed to support the outdoor education programs along with volunteers and students who work in the giving garden, orchard, and native plant nursery. The outdoor classroom will provide much-needed respite from the weather while serving as a gathering space for tours, events, and general guest services. By powering itself and capturing its own water, the building will be an instructional tool and demonstrative of green technologies. To date, $278,000 in grant funds have been secured, although considerably more funding is required to complete the outdoor classroom project.

To honor all sources of major funding, the Conservancy created the Donor Wall of Honor at Wakamatsu Farm in June 2018. The Donor Wall started with the names of ninety-one major donors who have significantly contributed to the Farm dating back to the beginning of the acquisition efforts. The panels have ample room for many more names of individuals and businesses who will contribute to the preservation, care, and development of landmark Wakamatsu Farm in the future.

Each year, the number of people who benefit from the Farm steadily grows. Each year since the acquisition, more and more volunteers and visitors appreciate the unfolding story of a landmark Farm, which is so significant to Japanese-Americans and their immigration story. Still and oddly enough, most people have never heard of the place, including most locals. The secrecy may be the result of the Veerkamp's nearly 140 years of private ownership when random visitors were discouraged or forbidden access. Visitors often explain to the Conservancy how, in years past, they jumped the fence to visit the grave of Okei-san, the legendary "Japanese princess." These days, the public is welcome to enjoy Wakamatsu Farm during regularly scheduled events and tours found online at ARConservancy.org/wakamatsu.

As outreach, ARC offers many yearly public programs to share the Farm's history, including three prior festivals. ARC is currently working to secure sponsors, performers, speakers, vendors, scholars, and the like for its biggest festival ever. During four days, *WakamatsuFest150* on June 6 through 9 of 2019 will be the one-and-only sesquicentennial celebration at Wakamatsu Farm. Honoring the legacy of the Wakamatsu Colony on the exact date of its 150th anniversary is not only a chance to attract attention to the Farm; it is also an honorable obligation and a spectacular excuse to have fun. With fitting fanfare, the Conservancy will be prepared to host at least four thousand visitors to celebrate 150 years of Japanese American heritage, arts, and cuisine at *WakamatsuFest150*. This grand event, along with all other events, are intended to build up the property to become a "destination farm" where visitors of all ages will come from near and far to enjoy an assortment of fun, engaging, and rewarding experiences.

Many people who visit the Farm are intrigued not only by its nature and history. They are fascinated by the mysteries left behind by the colonists. Some unanswered questions include: What happened to Schnell and his family, especially Mary Schnell, who was the first known Japanese-American child? Who were the other Colonists, especially those in the historic photos? How many Colonists came, and what became of them all? How and when did Schnell organize all the crops for transport? What type of tea did they grow? Does any other Japanese Colony predate Wakamatsu Farm, or is it the first Japanese Colony in the world? What should be the long-term future of the Farm? Will an honored Japanese-American organization step up to claim the Farm and manage its future? As with Dr. Metraux's written work, ARC welcomes and appreciates further inquiry, exploration, and publications about the cultural, natural, agricultural, and related aspects of Wakamatsu Farm.

ARC describes Wakamatsu Farm as a "community place to experience natural resources, sustainable agriculture, and cultural history." But a place cannot be fully understood through words. A place is more fully understood through experience. When people experience Wakamatsu Farm, they see rolling hills, abundant trees, and grasses bedecked in seasonal colors. They hear birds, crickets, and cows. They admire the wildlife and the stars. They appreciate the ponds and streams. They smell the fresh, clean air. They delight in a fantastic story. They eat something wholesome and delicious. The touch the earth. Most visitors feel more relaxed, more at peace. Usually they are more joyful. Enchanting places have this sort of effect on people as history unfolds around them.

For now, ARC is the land's keeper, taking the time to restore and protect an important heritage site. ARC will continue to conserve and steward the land, repair and improve the Farm's infrastructure, and welcome and educate visitors and volunteers of all ages from around the world. Perhaps you have been fortunate enough to visit Wakamatsu Farm, or one day you will be honored to share its compelling history. Whether or not you visit, ARC hopes you will share the Wakamatsu Farm story with others.

Appendix I

Application to Place the Wakamatsu Colony Farm on the National Register of Historic Places in 2009

WAKAMATSU TEA AND SILK COLONY FARM
GOLD HILL (VICINITY), EL DORADO COUNTY
STAFF EVALUATION

The site of the Wakamatsu Tea and Silk Colony Farm is an intact rural historic landscape located near Gold Hill, approximately 2 miles south of the town of Coloma, where gold was discovered in California. The nominated property encompasses 54.3 acres. Contributing resources include a residence and barn associated with the Wakamatsu settlers, and landscape elements including mulberry trees (for sericulture) planted by the colonists, and associated agricultural fields and pond. The barn and house are adjacent to Cold Springs Road, the central road running through the town of Gold Hill. Expansive agricultural fields and rolling hills surround the buildings on all sides, including the lands west of the road. The nominated acreage maintains sufficient physical integrity and integrity of rural setting to convey the history of the Wakamatsu Colony.

The Wakamatsu Tea and Silk Colony Farm site is eligible for listing in the National Register under Criterion A at a national level of significance in the areas of ethnic heritage, agriculture, and early settlement. In 1869, on behalf of Matsudaira Katamori (a *daimyo* of the Tokugawa family), agent John Henry Schnell purchased land and buildings from Charles Graner to establish the Wakamatsu Tea and Silk Colony. Japanese colonists planted and maintained mulberry trees and silkworm cocoons for silk farming, as well as tea plants and seeds. It is one of the oldest properties in North

America associated with Japanese permanent settlement in the United States. The Wakamatsu colonists occupied the site from the summer of 1869 to the spring of 1871, and were a critical portent of the Japanese immigration to come in the last decades of the nineteenth century. Of the 55 people of Japanese heritage documented by a U.S. census in 1870, 22 were settled at the Wakamatsu Colony in Gold Hill. Mary Schnell, the daughter of Jou and John Henry Schnell, was two months old at the time of the census, and the first child of a Japanese immigrant born in the United States. In the area of Agriculture, the contributions of the colony mark the beginning of Japanese influence on the agricultural economy of California and the United States, particularly in the area of crop specialization. The contributions of the colony to California's agricultural industry are tied culturally to their Japanese heritage and include a focus on sericulture and tea, Japan's two most important export industries during the period of significance.

Rebecca Allen, Past Forward, Inc. prepared the nomination for the American River Conservancy. The property owner, the El Dorado County Board of Supervisors, the Japanese American Citizens League, and the National Japanese American Historical Society among others support the nomination. Staff visited the site on January 22, 2009.

Staff recommends the State Historical Resources Commission determine that the Wakamatsu Tea and Silk Colony Farm meets National Register Criterion A at the national level of significance and recommend the State Historic Preservation Officer approve the nomination for forwarding to the National Park Service for listing in the National Register.

Cynthia Toffelmier, M.A.
Historian II
March 17, 2009

NATIONAL REGISTER OF HISTORIC PLACES CONTINUATION SHEET

Narrative Description

The site of the Wakamatsu Tea and Silk Colony Farm is an intact rural landscape, located in Gold Hill, approximately 2 miles south of the town of Coloma, where gold was discovered in California. Although near the gold fields, local farms dominated the Gold Hill area. In 1869, on behalf of Matsudaira Katamori (a daimyo of the Tokugawa family), agent John Henry Schnell purchased land and buildings from Charles Graner to establish the Wakamatsu Tea and Silk Colony. Japanese colonists planted and maintained mulberry trees and silkworm cocoons for silk farming, as well as tea plants and seeds. Dominant features of the landscape that convey the history of the short-lived colony are a residence, barn, associated vegetation, small pond, and expansive agricultural fields.

The residence was built by the original owner (Graner) and may date as early as 1856; physical evidence found in the basement suggests that Graner expanded the building to its current configuration during his tenure. The house is a simple two-story rectangular (58 ft. north-south by 48 ft. east-west) gable-roof farmhouse with a wraparound porch and a lean-to addition on the north side. There is a full basement, where the dressed stone foundation construction can be seen. The house is wood-framed; full dimension lumber and square nails are evident. The 10 ft. wide covered porch dominates the south, west, and north elevations. The main entrance is on the west elevation: the downstairs has a center door with a set of two windows flanking the entrance; three evenly spaced windows dominate the top floor. There is a 1950s era extended gable rear addition placed on the east side; original exterior building elements are visible on the interior. Overall, the exterior of the building maintains excellent historical integrity. The bottom interior of the house has been modified, although many original elements remain; the interior of the second floor is divided into several small sleeping rooms, and appears to retain much of its historical integrity.

The barn is north of the main house; it measures 68 1/2 ft. north-south by 65 1/2 ft. east-west. It is roughly square building with a multipitched gable roof of corrugated iron over wood shingles. The wood-framed structure is covered with V-rustic siding, and is of post construction on a rock foundation. The floor is of tongue and groove construction. Full dimension lumber was used in its construction, and many main structural elements show mortise and tenon cutouts; square cut nails are also evident. The building has been remodeled on the exterior and interior; original lumber was used but evidence of wire nails suggests a later structural strengthening and remodeling for use as a dairy barn.

Other vegetative and physical evidence of the Wakamatsu Colony can still be seen in the local landscape. A large keaki (Zelcova) tree is next to the house and was planted by the Japanese colonists. The colonists also planted mulberries on the property to the east of the house and barn. The original mulberries have long since died, but approximately 10–12 volunteers remain, suggesting where the colonists conducted their sericulture experiments. During their first year on the property, Wakamatsu colonists excavated and filled a small pond for fish culture. The approximately 1/4 acre pond is found east of the barn; its size varies according to the rainfall. Agricultural lands surround the main house and barn, and extend to the west and east of the main cluster of structures. According to the contemporary newspaper accounts and an 1871 General Land Office Map, Schnell and the Wakamatsu colonists planted these fields with tea plants and a vineyard; while these specific plants are no longer grown, the property has remained as agricultural fields since that time. Comparison of the modern landscape with an 1883 lithograph shows that the physical appearance of the house, as well as the barn, and surrounding agricultural fields has remained remarkably intact.

In 1873, Francis Veerkamp purchased the Wakamatsu Colony lands. His descendants have owned the property since that time, maintained agricultural use of the property. Additional noncontributing buildings represent the tenure of the Veerkamp family. A small wood-framed rectangular (24 ft. x 12.5 ft.) tractor barn is between the primary residence and barn; based on its full dimension lumber, and possible correlation with the 1883 lithograph, it dates to the late nineteenth century. During the early twentieth century, use of the farm as a dairy, a long rectangular (68 ft. x 18 ft.) dairy barn and wood-framed residence (49.5 ft. x 24.5 ft.) were built behind (east) of the primary barn. A circa 1930s–1940s rectangular (18 ft. x 24.5 ft.) wood-framed garage was built just northeast of the main residence. Another 1950s residence (24 ft. x 28 ft.) was built east of the main residence, behind a small hill and not in the view shed of the historic structures. Two additional noncontributing outbuildings are directly across Cold Springs Road from the primary residence. One is small wood-framed rectangular shed (18 ft. x 16 ft.) that may have materials from the early twentieth century, but has been reconstructed. The second is a post-1940s rectangular (40 ft. x 60 ft.) shed.

Despite these later additions, the core of the Wakamatsu Colony lands retains integrity of their rural setting. The barn and house are adjacent to Cold Springs Road, the central road running through the town of Gold Hill. As during the tenure of the colony, expansive agricultural fields and rolling hills surround the buildings on all sides, including the lands west of the road. In addition, the vegetation and small pond convey the setting when the colonists occupied the land.

Statement of Significance

The Wakamatsu Tea and Silk Colony site is eligible for listing in the National Register under Criterion A at a national level of significance in the areas of ethnic heritage, agriculture, and early settlement. It is one of the oldest properties in North America associated with Japanese permanent settlement in the United States. Members of the colony occupied the site from 1869–1871. The site has a residence and barn associated with the Wakamatsu settlers, mulberry trees (for sericulture) planted by the colonists, and associated agricultural fields and pond. The agricultural setting, including surrounding farmlands, has remarkable integrity, maintaining its rural setting. Overall, the site represents the vanguard of Japanese American contributions to the culture of the United States.

The Wakamatsu Tea and Silk Colony contributes significantly to the broader patterns of the nation's history under the themes of Ethnic Heritage and Exploration/Settlement as the site of the first permanent settlement of Japanese immigrants in the continental United States. The Wakamatsu colonists occupied the site from the summer of 1869 to the spring of 1871, and were a critical portent of the Japanese immigration to come in the last decades of the nineteenth century. Of the 55 people of Japanese heritage documented by a U.S. census in 1870, 22 were settled at the Wakamatsu Colony in Gold Hill. The added uniqueness of some of the Wakamatsu colonists, members of the Japanese samurai (military) class, adds another level of importance, the ethnic heritage of the site. Mary Schnell, the daughter of Jou and John Henry Schnell, was two months old at the time of the census, and the first child of a Japanese immigrant born in the United States. During the dedication of the California Historical Landmark plaque, the year 1969 was designated as the centennial of the Japanese immigration to the United States.

The contributions of the colony to California's agricultural industry are tied culturally to their Japanese heritage and include a focus on sericulture and tea, Japan's two most important export industries at the time the colony was established. While some prior experimentation with tea and silk farming had been attempted (by non-Japanese) in California, these efforts met with little success. Under the theme of Agriculture, the contributions of the Colony to the agriculture industry are recognized; they mark the beginning of Japanese influence on the agricultural economy of California and the United States. The Japanese colonists, like the later Japanese immigrants of the 1880s and 1890s, made significant contributions to the agricultural development and crop specialization, particularly in the western United States. For nearly a century and a half, the integrity of the rural agricultural setting of the Colony has been maintained, including the residence occupied by colonists and the native trees that they planted.

Historical Context

To understand the significance of the Wakamatsu Tea and Silk Colony, it is important to highlight the context of Japanese society that the immigrants were fleeing. Beginning in the early seventeenth century, Tokugawa shogunates emphasized cultural isolation and prohibited Japanese citizens from traveling abroad. This isolationist doctrine remained in place until Commodore William Perry, acting for United States, forced open several Japanese ports to U.S. trade in 1853–1854.

In the 1860s, the cultural isolation was faltering. Matsudaira Katmori (1835–1893) was distantly related to the Tokugawa family and was a daimyo (local lord) of the Aizu Wakamatsu province. Matsudaira disagreed with the Tokugawa policy of isolation, and instead chose to walk a line between "Eastern ethics, Western science." John Henry Schnell and his brother were arms dealers in Japan, and also dabbled in merchandizing other Japanese goods. Matsudaira was one of the Schnell's best customers, and the brothers trained Matsudaira's samurais in the use of firearms. Matsudaira's relationship with Schnell was close enough that he gave him an honorary Japanese name that included two of same kanji characters as were in Matsudaira's name. Schnell married a Japanese samurai class woman. Strife between the Tokugawa faction and those who propped up the Emperor for their own benefit resulted in civil war, ultimately leading to the Meiji Restoration, as well as Matsudaira's surrender in 1868 (Van Sant 2000, 119–23). Matsudaira was condemned for execution.

After Matsudaira surrendered, the Schnell brothers were in jeopardy. John Henry Schnell, his Japanese wife Jou, and six other Japanese colonists left Japan on May 20, 1869, and arrived in San Francisco seven days later. Schnell intended to purchase lands on behalf of Matsudaira, who thought he may need a place of exile. Schnell was to establish an agricultural colony that would grow tea and mulberry trees, and cultivate silkworms. Schnell chose California as their destination as the state of California (beginning in 1866) used government financing to entice farmers to speculate with sericulture (Starns 1993, 86). Parasitic epidemics had destroyed much of the lucrative European sericulture, and many areas were trying to take advantage of this lucrative export trade (Van Sant 2000, 124). The 1869 arrival of the colonists received the attention of the San Francisco newspaper *Alta California*, as Japanese immigrants were a relative rarity in the United States.

Prior to the arrival of Schnell's group, there were only a handful of Japanese who came to the continental United States (the history of Japanese influence on Hawaii is complex, and not considered here, as Hawaii did not formally become part of the United States until 1959). Van Sant (2000) suggests that the first two Japanese arrivals were castaway sailors, who arrived in the 1840s, and eventually returned to Japan. In 1860, the Japanese Tokugawa shogunate established an embassy in the United States, and staffed it with 77 members; their stay in the United States was temporary. In 1864, a young Japanese man stowed away on a merchant ship, eventually making his way to Massachusetts. There, he became a student and converted to Christianity, returning to Japan as an influential missionary in 1874. A few overseas students (*ryūgakusei*) attended colleges in the west, including two who attended Rutgers University in 1866. More came later to study at Rutgers; with the exception of five students who died, all returned to Japan. In 1867, six young Japanese samurai men joined the utopian community in upstate New York, known as the Brotherhood of New Life. They had met the charismatic leader of the commune two years earlier, while in England to study Western science and technology. When Civil War erupted in 1868, the six left for Japan, accompanied by several other Japanese who had also come to the commune. Other than these few stories, specific knowledge about the presence of Japanese in the United States prior to 1869 is limited, in part because U.S. census records did not record the Japanese at the embassy, nor did they count temporary visitors, including merchants and other officials.

The Wakamatsu colonists were different from previous Japanese visitors to the continental United States because they intended to permanently settle in California, in contrast to Japanese students, merchants, and diplomats. It was the rarity of this group of Japanese immigrants that caught the attention of the San Francisco *Alta California* newspaper, which noted that the colonists brought means for their agricultural productivity with them, including "50,000 three year old kuwa [mulberry] trees" used for sericulture, and that 6 million tea seeds would soon be sent to them (Van Sant 2000, 124). The newspaper praised the Japanese work ethic, as well as Jou Schnell's beauty and grace. This was an attitude in contrast to the more prevalent discrimination toward Chinese miners, perhaps because the Wakamatsu colonists cultivated Japanese plants, so that the threat of direct economic competition was generally not perceived.

To establish the Wakamatsu Colony, John Henry Schnell purchased two parcels of land in the town of Gold Hill, near Coloma (where gold was discovered) from Charles Graner on 18 June 1869. He also purchased a third interest in a nearby quarry, south of the town of Gold Hill. The history of these lands is complicated, as not all land transactions were recorded at the El Dorado County Recorder's Office. Graner had purchased 160 acres of land from Samuel and Mary Hill in 1856; the Hills had preempted and filed a claim for the land, in anticipation of patenting the land at a later date. Graner already settled an odd-shaped smaller piece of land adjoining the southern border of the Hill property. Although his legal preemption is not on file at the Recorder's Office, Graner claimed the land, and constructed a house and barn on the smaller piece of land. The Graners sold two acres of this property to the local district in 1868, creating an irregular southern boundary. To further complicate interpretation of land ownership, property boundaries somewhat shifted to the south and west in 1871, when the Government Land Office officially surveyed the land. Through study of neighboring claims, physical survey (Willson 2009), and some approximation, it can be closely estimated that the size of the two parcels of land that Schnell purchased was around 180 acres. Because of the complexity of land transactions, there is confusion in the published literature over the size of the original property. Starns (1993, 89–90) lists the acreage as 160, but she noted that Schnell reported to the *Alta California* that he had more than 600 acres under cultivation. Van Sant (2000, 125) lists the acreage as 640 acres.

It is possible that Schnell's report may have been misconstrued, as the Japanese measurement of 640 tan is equivalent to about 160 acres. Alternatively, Schnell may have embellished. Schnell's report to the newspaper about the size and equipment at the Colony was expansive: he claimed a "large orchard, thousands of bearing vines, grain fields, a good brick [sic] house well furnished, a barn, well-appointed wine house, implements of husbandry, horses, wagons, cows, pigs, fowls, and good and abundant water" (Starns 1993, 90). It is difficult to tell how much Schnell was hoping for and what he understood from Graner, as he had yet seen the property. Schnell's purchase certainly included a house, barn, and fields.

In any case, once at the Colony site, the colonists quickly went to work, establishing their farm, planting mulberry trees, oil plants, and constructing a pond for breeding fish. Schnell successfully displayed silk cocoons at the 1869 California State Agricultural Fair in Sacramento. In March 1870, a California newspaper noted that the colonists had received and planted more than 140,000 tea plants. The tea plants were likely planted in the flat fields west of the main residence and barn.

During the fall of 1869, and summer of 1870, at least 26 more Japanese colonists came to join the Wakamatsu Farm. Some of the colonists were farmers, some skilled workers such as a carpenter, and some were of the lower samurai class. According to the 1870 U.S. census, there were 55 Japanese in the United States. Of these, 22 were colonists at Wakamatsu: 14 men, 6 women, and 2 children. The two children were Schnell's daughters, one born in Japan, and one at the Wakamatsu site. Van Sant (2000, 125) estimates that the number of Japanese colonists at Wakamatsu was more likely 35, by far the largest grouping of Japanese settlers in the United States at that time.

At the 1870 Horticultural Fair in San Francisco, Schnell and two colonists displayed tea plants and silkworms. The colonists also planted grapevines and the 1870 census lists Fred Dielbol, a Swiss winemaker, present at the Colony. The 1871 General Land Office map makes note of "Schnell's Vineyard." The local newspaper, the *Mountain Democrat*, praised the industriousness of the Japanese colonists (Starns 1993, 93; Van Sant 2000, 126–27).

The Wakamatsu Tea and Silk Colony Farm was destined to be short-lived. Many factors contributed to the Colony's collapse: temporary drought, competition for water with local miners who "jumped claim," poor management skills, and the withdrawal of financial support from Matsudaira. Surprisingly, the new Meiji government pardoned Matsudaira; he chose to become a Shinto priest and remain in Japan. A short but ill-timed drought caused the tea plants to wither and die. To make matters worse, a few local miners diverted water from a stream on the property. Documents at the Recorder's Office show that Schnell was in legal trouble regarding the land ownership by the end of December, 1870. In June 1871, Schnell left California, along with his wife Jou, and their two daughters. Although he promised to return, he did not, effectively abandoning the other Japanese colonists. According to Sioli (1883, 112), whose source was likely Francis Veerkamp, Schnell was killed after he returned to Japan.

The fate of only three of the colonists is specifically known. Matsunosuke Sakurai, likely a former samurai, worked for the Veerkamp family who had purchased the Wakamatsu lands in 1873. According to Veerkamp family oral tradition, he was a "wonderful gardener" and friend of the family (Yohalem 1977, 220). Matsunosuke lived in Gold Hill until his death in 1901. Okei, a young nursemaid for the Schnells, also stayed with the Veerkamp family. She died at age 19 in 1871, and is buried on Veerkamp property, nearby (but outside of) the Wakamatsu property. Her gravesite is still maintained by members of the local Japanese American community, and a replica of her gravesite has been created in Aizu Wakamatsu, Japan. Masumizu Kuninosuke, a young carpenter, moved to nearby Coloma and became a farmer and miner. He married Carrie Wilson, a woman of African and American Indian descent, in 1877. He and his family eventually moved to Sacramento. Masumizu Kuninosuke died in 1915, at the age of 66. His descendants remain in the area and were interrogated by the FBI in the 1940s (during World War II) to determine if they should be classified as "enemy aliens" (they were not). As for the others, some traveled to, and stayed in, San Francisco. Only a few possibly returned to Japan; records are scarce because they would have been considered enemies of the Meiji government (Van Sant 2000, 128–29).

Although it was short-lived (1869–1871), the Colony had an effect on U.S. agricultural traditions. The colonists themselves were the vanguard of Japanese Issei (first-generation Japanese immigrants) into the United States. Large numbers of Japanese began to arrive on U.S. mainland in the 1880s. The Meiji restoration had brought an end to Civil War, but it also began a period of rapid modernization, due to contact with the Western world. The resulting social upheaval caused many to look for new places to settle and continue their traditional agricultural practices. Many of the Issei adopted the agricultural colony model as a mechanism for maintaining their cultural connections. By 1900, there were more than 24,000 Japanese living in the continental United States (Daniels 1988, 115). Most lived in the western states, and their effect on local agriculture was profound (Daniels 1988, 143); in California, for example more than 10 percent of all California farm products were produced by Japanese Americans (Van Sant 2000, 129). As Daniels (in Van Sant 2000, x) notes, the story of the earliest Japanese immigrants highlights the facets of multiculturalism in the United States. The National Park Service commissioned Five Views, An Ethnic Site Survey for California, intended to celebrate and highlight the country's ethnic diversity; the story of the Wakamatsu Tea and Silk Colony Farm is featured in the section on Japanese American heritage.

In 1924, a resurgence of interest in the Wakamatsu story began. Late attorney and Sacramento Japanese American community leader Henry Taketa interviewed Henry Veerkamp, who was one year older than Okei, and 75 at the time of the interview (Taguma 2007). Local Japanese Americans started to tend Okei's gravesite, and the story of the Wakamatsu Colony reemerged. In 1969, then Governor Ronald Reagan proclaimed the Wakamatsu Colony site to be a California Historical Landmark No. 815. The Japanese American Citizens League and the Japanese Consul General Shima Seiichi supported the proclamation. Matsudaira Ichiro, the grandson of the colonist's daimyo financier, also attended the ceremony. The Japanese American community designated 1969 as the Japanese American centennial. In 1986, Yoshiki Inomata, the Mayor of Aiza Wakamatsu, Japan wrote a letter of thanks to Malcolm Veekamp, praising the family for their care of the gravesite. In 2001, the Veerkamp family donated an original Wakamatsu banner with the Colony's lotus blossom crest, and a ceremonial dagger (possibly a short samurai sword) that may have belonged to Jou Schnell to the nearby Marshall Gold Discovery State Historic Park. In 2007, a Veerkamp descendant found photographs of the colonists in an envelope; the photographs were taken at an historically known photography studio in Placerville, California.

When Francis and Louisa Veerkamp purchased the Wakamatsu Colony lands in 1873, they blended local and national history. The Veerkamps had settled in Gold Hill in 1852, and purchased land adjacent to the Colony and in nearby communities to settle their six sons. The Veerkamp family maintained the rural agricultural nature of the property, preserving the heritage and landscape of the Wakamatsu Colony. Through many complicated land transactions, the Wakamatsu lands have passed to several Veerkamp sons and daughters of subsequent generations. The Helen L. Veerkamp Revocable Trust (Gary Veerkamp, Trustee) currently holds approximately 127 acres of the original approximate 180 acres of the Wakamatsu Colony lands; they also hold much adjoining acreage. The 54.3 acres included in this nomination constitute the heart of the Colony, centered on the main structures, mulberry plantings, pond, vineyard, and surrounding flat agricultural lands to convey the rural setting of the Colony farmlands. The association of the Wakamatsu Colony with the remaining acreage is not as immediately apparent, although archaeological survey and investigation may enhance the association. The remaining acreage (outside of the nominated 54.3 acres) has retained its agricultural setting, but is comprised of more rolling hills that are less likely to have been farmed by the Wakamatsu colonists, and has been further influenced by cattle grazing and the early twentieth-century construction of a small 6-acre lake.

The American River Conservancy currently leases portions of the land from the Helen Veerkamp Trust. The Conservancy's intention is to preserve the site, rehabilitate the structures, and to identify appropriate governmental partners to develop an historical park celebrating the heritage of the Wakamatsu Tea and Silk Colony Farm. *Nichi Bei Times*, Northern California's oldest Japanese American newspaper, has recently published an article supporting these efforts (Taguma 2007). The National Japanese American Historical Society, the Japanese American Citizens League (Florin, Placer, Sacramento and National Chapters), Congresswoman Doris Matsui, Assemblyman Alan Nakanishi, El Dorado County Supervisor Ron Briggs, the El Dorado County Chamber of Commerce, and many others public figures and private citizens also support this preservation effort.

Appendix II

Text of the Deed of the Sale of Land by Charles M. Graner to J. Henry Schnell

June 18, 1869

This Indenture made the Eighteenth day of June of our Lord One Thousand Eight Hundred and Sixty Nine. Between Charles M. Graner of the County of Eldorado and State of California of the first part and J. Henry Schnell the party of the Second part. Witnesseth That the Said party of the first part for and in consideration of the Sum of Five Thousand Dollars of the United States of America to him in hand paid by the said party of the Second part the receipt whereof is hereby acknowledged. Was granted bargained and sold. And Conveyed. And by these presents does grant bargain. Sell and convey unto the Said party of the Second Part and to his heirs and assigns forever. All of the following described property situated in Coloma Township County of El Dorado and State of California.

Commencing at the South east corner of Mr. Moseley's Ranch known as the Bay state Ranch in Gold Hill precinct hence running East one Hundred and sixty rods South to a stake and stone hence running East one hundred and sixty rods South to a white oak tree marked H.H. now cut down, thence north One hundred and sixty rods to a white oak tree marked "H" then One hundred and sixty rods to the place of beginning.

Also that certain piece or parcel of land lying and being near the village of Gold Hill in the County of El Dorado and State of California. And bounded as follows in the South and West by the ranches of H. D. Newell, and Charles M. Graner, herein-before described and in the north and east by the ranches of Richard Price, Robert McKay and on the East by the ranch of Henry Teeney" and on the south by the ranch of ___ Kesttering.

Also the one undivided interest in a certain Stone Quarry lying immediately East of said Village of Gold Hill in the County and State aforesaid the other two thirds undivided interest being owned by Michael Marquart and John Brown, the first described price of land contains about 160 acres of land, more or less.

Together with all and Singular tenements, hereditaments and appurtenances thereunto belonging, or in any wise appertaining, and the reversion, and reversions, and remainder and remainders rents issues and profits thereof. And also all the estate right title and interest property possession claim and demand whatsoever. As well in law as in equity of the said party of the first part of in or to the said premises. And every part and parcel thereof with the appurtenances To Have and to Hold all and Singular.

The Said Premises together with the appurtenances unto the Said party of the second part his heirs and assigns forever.

In witness whereof, the Said party of the second part his heirs and assigns forever. In witness whereof, the Said party of the first part has hereinto Set his hand and seal the day and year first afore written (Ver Kamp $500 Chas Graner Jn 18th 1869).

Charles M. Graner (and seal)

Bibliography

Ahmad, Diana. *The Opium Debate and Chinese Exclusion Laws in the Nineteenth-Century American West*. Reno and Las Vegas: University of Nevada Press, 2007.
American River Conservancy. *The Wakamatsu Tea & Silk Colony Farm: America's First Issei*. Pamphlet: 2012
Azuma, Eiichiro. *Between Two Empires: Race, History, and Transnationalism in Japanese America*. New York: Oxford University Press, 2005.
———. "'Pioneers of Overseas Japanese Development': Japanese American History and the Making of Expansionist Orthodoxy in Imperial Japan." *Journal of Asian Studies* 67, no. 4 (2008): 1187–1226.
Barsotti, Joan Barton. *Okei-San: A Girl's Journey, Japan to California, 1868–1871*. Camino CA: Barsotti Books, 2006.
Beasley, W. G. *The Meiji Restoration*. Stanford CA: Stanford University Press, 1972.
Chang, Gordon et al. *Before Internment: Essays in Prewar Japanese-American History*. Stanford: Stanford University Press, 2006.
Clark, E. Warren. *Life and Adventure in Japan*. New York: American Tract Society, 1878.
Cwiertka, Katazina Joanna. *Modern Japanese Cuisine: Food, Power and National Identity*. New York: Reaktion Books, 2015.
Daniels, Roger. *Asian America: Chinese and Japanese in the United States Since 1850*. Seattle: University of Washington Press, 1988.
Dunk, Nancy. *At the Heart of Gold Country: Placerville and Its Surrounding Area*. Placerville: El Dorado County Historical Society, 2013.
Duus, Peter. *The Rise of Modern Japan*. New York: Houghton Mifflin, 1976.
El Dorado County Recorder's Office, El Dorado County, CA var. Preemption and land ownership records.
Gorō, Shiba. *Remembering Aizu: The Testament of Shiba Gorō*. Honolulu: University of Hawaii Press, 1999.
Griffis, William Elliot. *The Mikado's Empire: History of Japan and Personal Experiences, Observations and Studies in Japan 1870–1874*. New York: Harper & Brothers, 1883.
Guglieri, Wendy. "Ofuji Matsugoro, Wakamatsu Colonist." *Newsletter of the American River Conservancy,* January 2016.
Guinn, J. M. "Some Early California Industries That Failed." *Annual Publication of the Historical Society of Southern California*, July 1907.
Huffman, James. *Down and Out in Late Meiji Japan*. Honolulu: Hawaii University Press, 2018.
Inomata, Yoshiki. Letter to Malcom Veerkamp. Mayor of Aizuwakamatsu City. National Park Service, 2006.
Lee, Erika. *The Making of Asian America: A History*. New York: Simon & Schuster, 2015.

Lee, K. W. "Gold Hill Colony: Hope and Betrayal for a 'Mayflower.'" *Nichi Bei Times*, January 1, 2011.
Leung, Peter C. Y. *One Day, One Dollar: The Chinese Farming Experience in the Sacramento River Delta, California*. Taipei: The Liberal Arts Press, 1993.
Meissner, Kurt. "General Eduard Schnell." *Monumenta Nipponica* 4, no. 2 (1941): 395–427.
Nagai, Mariko. "And They Crossed the Ocean." *Wakamatsu Farm News*, Spring 2017.
Nakanishi, Don T. "Japanese Americans." In the *Kodansha Encyclopedia of Japan*, Volume 4, 13–17. Tokyo: Kodansha, 1983.
National Park Service. *A History of Japanese. Americans in California. Part of Five Views, An Ethnic Site Survey for California*. 2004. Online book found at nps.gov/history/history/online_books/5views/5views4a.htm.
Nimura, Janice P. *Daughters of the Samurai: A Journey from East to West and Back*. New York: W. W. Norton & Co., 2015.
Pfaezler, Jean. *Driven Out: The Forgotten War against Chinese Americans*. New York: Random House, 2007.
Quero, Hugo Cordova. *Transnational Faiths: Latin American Immigrants and Their Religions in Japan*. Farnham, UK: Ashgate, 2014.
Saaler, Sven, and Kudo Akira, eds. *Mutual Perceptions and Images in Japanese-German Relations*. Leiden: Brill, 2017.
Sederquist, Betty. *Coloma: Images of America*. Charleston, SC: Arcadia Publishing, 2012.
Sioli, Paolo. *Historical Souvenir of El Dorado County, California*. Oakland, CA: Paolo Sioli, 1883. Reprint, Georgetown, CA: Cedar Ridge Publishing, 1998.
Spickard, Paul. *Japanese Americans: The Formation and Transformations of an Ethnic Group*. New York: Twayne Publishers, 1996.
Starns, Jean E. *Gold Hill: Bonds of Time, Families & Land*. Fairfield, CA: James Stevenson, 1993.
Starr, Kevin. "The Wakamatsu Tea and Silk Farm at Gold Hill." Accessed February 17, 2017. http://calrice.org/pdf/WakamatsuKevinStarr.pdf.
State of California, Executive Department. "Proclamation by Governor Ronald Reagan." Sacramento: California State Archives, February 3, 1969.
Taguma, Kenji G. "Where it all Began: Preserving the First Settlement of Japanese in America." *Nichi Bei Times* (San Francisco, CA), April 26, 2007. Available at Nichibeitimes.com.
Takaki, Ronald. *Strangers from a Different Shore: A History of Asian America*. New York: Back Bay Books, 1998.
Takuma, Kenji G. "Where It All Began: Preserving the First Settlement of Japanese Americans." *Nichi Bei Times*, April 26, 2007.
Tanaka, Akira. "Boshin Civil War." In the *Kodansha Encyclopedia of Japan*. Tokyo: Kodansha, 1983.
Tanimoto, Herb. "Honoring Matsunosuke Sakurai." *Wakamatsu Farm News*, Spring 2017.
———. *Keiko's Kimono: A Doll's Journey to America in 1869 with the Wakamatsu Tea and Silk Colony*. Sacramento: I Street Press, 2016.
Torimoto, Ikuko. *Okina Kyūin and the Politics of Early Japanese Immigration to the United States, 1868–1924*. Jefferson, NC: McFarland Publishing, 2016.
Totman, Conrad. *The Collapse of the Tokugawa Bakufu*. Honolulu: University of Hawaii Press, 1980.
Van Sant, John E. *Pacific Pioneers: Japanese Journeys to America and Hawaii, 1850–80*. Urbana and Chicago: University of Illinois Press, 2000.
Wildie, Kevin. *Sacramento's Historic Japantown: Legacy of a Lost Neighborhood*. Charleston, SC: The History Press, 2013.
Willson, James E. Letter to Rebecca Allen, 13 March 2009. Licensed land surveyor, Carlton Engineering.
Wright, Diana E. "Female Combatants and Japan's Meiji Restoration: The Case of Aizu." *War in History* 8, no. 4 (2001): 396–417.
Yohalem, Betty. *Stories and Pictures of El Dorado Pioneer Families*. Placerville: Eldorado Chamber of Commerce, 1977.

NEWSPAPERS

Daily Alta California, February 24, 1869.
———, May 21, 1869.
———, May 27, 1869.
———, June 3, 1869.
———, June 7, 1869.
———, June 8, 1869.
———, June 14, 1869.
———, June 16, 1869.
———, July 3, 1869.
———, July 30, 1869.
———, August 15, 1869.
———, October 22, 1869.
———, October 24, 1869.
———, June 27, 1870.
———, July 13, 1870.
———, September 2, 1870.
———, September 4, 1870.
———, September 5, 1870.
———, April 3, 1871.
———, August 6, 1871.
Daily Morning Call, January 1, 1870.
———, January 2, 1870.
———, January 3, 1870.
Daily Evening Bulletin, February 9, 1871.
The London and China Telegraph, November 6, 1867.
Los Angeles Times, June 10, 2007.
Mountain Democrat, October 2, 1869.
———, May 10, 2013.
Pacific Rural Press, February 18, 1871.
———, April 15, 1871.
———, February 15, 1879.
Sacramento Daily Union, May 28, 1869.
———, June 18, 1869.
———, June 19, 1869.
———, June 5, 1869.
———, June 19, 1869.
———, July 31, 1869.
———, September 18, 1869.
———, March 2, 1870.
———, December 31, 1870.
San Francisco Call, March 20, 1893.

Index

Abiko, Kyutaro, 104
agriculture: ARC and, 116–117; in California, 44, 53, 65–67, 75n6, 129; colony progress with, 73–75; Japanese immigrants and, 44, 129; Kimura on, 97; and landscape, 54–55; National Register on, 8–9
Aizu Domain (Aizu Han), 5; Boshin War and, 17, 18, 20–21, 22; characteristics of, 23; climate of, 84; and exile, 25–26, 27; fall of, 23–26; military code of conduct, 23; Okei tombstone replica in, 95; Schnell and, 31–34; Shiba on, 26–27; and silk production, 69
Allen, Rebecca, 122
Amanin, 57
American reactions to Japanese immigrants: versus Chinese immigrants, 39, 49, 59; to later waves of immigration, 8; scale of immigration and, 40, 42–46; to Wakamatsu colonists, 7–8, 39–40, 46–49
American River Conservancy (ARC), 4, 7, 12, 113–119; mission, 114; volunteers, 117, 118; on water contamination, 85, 114–115
Amesabra, 57
arms trade: and Boshin War, 22–23; Schnells and, 5, 32–33
Azuma, Eiichiro, 14, 95, 96–98

bamboo, 69, 72
banner found at Wakamatsu site, 34, 88, 89n13, 130
Barsotti, Joan Barton, 60, 98–99
Beasley, W. G., 14
Boshin War, 3, 5, 19; and Aizu Han, 23–26; historiography of, 14; Matsudaira and, 21–23
Briggs, Ron, 130
Brooks, Charles, 108
Brotherhood of New Life, 126
Byakko-tai, 24

California: agriculture in, 44, 53, 65–67, 125, 129; climate of, 35, 70, 84; economy of, 9; Gold Rush, 5, 11–12; Schnell and, 34–35; subsidies for agricultural projects, 80–81
California Cultural and Historical Endowment, 116
California Farmer and Journal of Useful Sciences, 67
California Industrial Commission Report, 46
Calistoga, 80, 88n5
canning process, 111
carpenters, 10, 57, 59, 87, 110
castaways, 42, 126
Census of 1870, 13, 36n1; on Wakamatsu Japanese, 56–57
cherry blossom trees, 117

139

China: and emigration, 5, 39, 41; immigrants from, American reactions to, 39, 49, 59; Opium War and, 19
China, PMSS, 52, 62n2
Choshu Domain, 19, 20, 21–22, 25, 27, 28n16
Christian missionaries, in Japan, 18
Claretie, Jules, 61
Clark, E. Warren, 42, 43
climate: of California, 35; and fate of colony, 79, 82, 83, 84; of Gold Hill, 11, 70, 71; and tea, 70
coffee cultivation, 75n6
Cold Springs, 54, 62n10
Coloma, 11, 57; Chinese immigrants in, 39; landscape of, 54–55, 115
cotton, 67, 68
Craig, Teruko, 26
creation stories, 1
Cwiertka, Katazina Joanna, 111

dagger found at Wakamatsu site, 88, 89n13, 130
Daidjiro family, 57
Daily Alta California, 14n8; on agricultural plans of colony, 56, 63n14, 69–70, 71–72, 76n22; on arrival of Japanese colonists, 46–48, 52, 53–54; on fate of colony, 79–80; on miners, 85; on progress of colony, 73, 78; on silk industry, 66
Daily Morning Call: on arrival of Japanese colonists, 48–49; on housing for laborers, 59–60; on labor relations, 35–36; on landscape of Coloma, 54–55; on progress of colony, 74
daimyo, 19; definition of, 28n1
dekaseginin, 41, 43
De Long, Charles, 28n16
Dielbol, Fred, 128
doctor, in Wakamatsu Colony, 49, 50n23
drought: in California, 35; and fate of colony, 83–85; and silk industry, 66
Duus, Peter, 22

economic issues: California and, 9; Japan and, 18–19, 67–69
Ehrgott, Alan, 115–116

El Dorado County, 11; landscape of, 53–55, 114
Elebeck, George, 111
exile of Aizu people, 25–26; Shiba on, 27

farmers: Japanese immigrants as, 40–41, 44. *See also* agriculture
festivals: Japanese, 101; at Wakamatsu, 103–105, 118
fish pond, 56, 72, 76n21
Fitts, Mike, 87
Flyzero, 57
frontier era, of Japanese immigration, 40, 41–42, 126–127
Fujioka, Shiro, 94
Fukuinkai, 108
Fukuzawa Yukichi, 96
funding issues: ARC and, 116; and fate of colony, 82, 83, 86

Gibson, Gene, 104
Golden Feather Tea Farm, 87
Gold Hill, 2, 6; Chinese immigrants in, 39; climate of, 11, 70, 71; landscape of, 11–12, 54–55, 62n11, 115
Gold Rush, 5, 11–12
Gold Trail Elementary School, 1, 98, 113
Graner, Charles, 10, 12, 56, 72, 127, 133–134
gravesite of Okei, 92–93, 96, 98, 99; Barsotti on, 98–99; Japanese replica of, 95, 103; as pilgrimage site, 2, 101–103
Griffis, William Elliot, 42, 43
Guinn, J. M., 75n6

Han, definition of, 28n1
Hansen, Art, 104
Hawaii, Japanese immigrants in, 41
Heco, Joseph, 42
Hill, Samuel and Mary, 12, 127
Hinds, William A., 61
Hokkaido, 21, 25
Hollister, colonel, 75n6
Honshu, 20, 25
Horticultural Fair, San Francisco, 1870, 73–74, 78

immigration: Miller on, ix. *See also* American reactions to Japanese

immigrants; Japanese immigration to United States
Inomata, Yoshiki, 130
Irwin, Robert W., 41
Issei historians of Japanese migration, 2, 4, 6; and Okei, 93–94
Ito, Okei (Okei-san), 2, 91–99; background of, 92–93; lack of knowledge on, 14, 91; later life, 6, 108–109, 129; remaking of story of, 2, 6, 14, 93–99. *See also* gravesite of Okei
Itogawa, Gene, 115
Iwakura Mission, 42

Jansen, Marius, 25
Japan: and age, 112; and agriculture, 67; climate of, 84; closed-door policy, 5, 18, 28n2; economic issues, 18–19, 67–69; and emigration, 3, 36; historical background, 17–27; and Okei, 96; Schnells in, 5–6, 13, 31–34, 52; and surnames, 63n15, 112; and taxation, 49n2; treaties, 19, 28n4, 68, 75n7; and United States, 46, 107
Japanese American Citizens League, 96
Japanese Americans: creation stories of, 2; importance of Wakamatsu Colony to, 7–9, 99, 124–125
Japanese immigration to United States, 2, 3–4, 39–49, 126–127; and agriculture, 44, 129; historical background, 5–7; *Issei* historians of, 2, 4, 6–7, 93–94; legal prohibitions and, 45–46; Miller on, ix; waves of, 40–41
Japanese women, 24; portrayal of, 95; at Vassar, 42
Japonisme, 61
journalists. *See* press
Junyaro, 57

kamon daimyo, 21; definition of, 28n7
Kawamura, Masahei, 95
keyaki (Japanese elm, *Zelkova serrata*), 75, 117, 123
Kimura Takeshi, 96–97
Kingdelryo, 57
Kintaro, 57
Kobata, Ronald, 105
Kochi, Fred, 95, 102

Komei, emperor of Japan, 19–20, 28n3

laborers, labor issues, 10, 35, 36, 58–59, 62, 86; and fate of colony, 80, 87; plan for, 70
Lee, Erika, 13, 45
Lee, K. W., 74
Li Po-Tai, 50n23
Lobach, Melissa, 113–119

Maeda, Wayne, 103, 105
Manchuria, 97–98
Marshall, James, 11
Masumizu, Kuninosuke, 57, 103, 111–112, 129
Matsudaira, Katamori: and Boshin War, 21–23; later life, 25, 28n16; rumors of association with colony, 34, 35, 51–52, 55, 82, 83; Schnells and, 32, 33, 58
Matsugoro family, 110
Matsui, Doris, 7, 130
Mead, Margaret, 1
media. *See* press
Meiji Restoration/Era, 17; and economy, 67–69; historiography of, 14; Shiba on, 26–27; term, 20
Meissner, Kurt, 13
Miller, Amy, ix–x
mining: Chinese immigrants and, 39; and landscape, 54–55; and water contamination, 85
mulberry trees, 6, 52, 58, 66, 67, 69, 71, 74
Mullen, John, 80
mysteries of Wakamatsu, 118–119; on Japanese colonists, 60–62; on Okei, 14, 91; and research, 12, 13, 14, 60–62; on Schnells, 13, 31, 52

Nagai, Mariko, 24
Nakahama, Manjiro, 42
Nakanishi, Alan, 130
National Register of Historic Places, 8–9, 121–130
Native Americans, in Gold Hill, 11, 115
newspapers. *See* press; *specific paper*
Nichi Bei Foundation, 103–105
Nichi Bei newspapers, 103–104, 130
Nihonmachi, 44
Nimura, Janice P., 24, 26

Nisenan native people, 11, 115
Nishijara Taro, 57

Ofuji, Matsugoko, 110–111
Okei-san. *See* Ito, Okei
"Okei's Lullaby," 92

Pacific Rural Press, 78–79, 80–81
Pakeyee, 57
Perry, Matthew, 18, 19, 43, 107
picture brides, 41, 44
pilgrimage: nature of, 101; Wakamatsu Farm as site of, 2, 101–105
pioneers, early Japanese immigrants as, 94, 95, 98
Placerville *Mountain Democrat*, 49, 73
press: on arrival of Japanese colonists, 46–49, 52, 53–54; on fate of colony, 78–79; on housing for laborers, 59–60; and Okei, 94–95; on progress of colony, 73–75; as research material, 13, 14n8; Schnell and, 82; and Wakamatsu colonists, 7–8, 60–61
prostitutes, early Japanese female immigrants as, 2, 95

Qing dynasty, 39

racial abuse, 42–43, 45, 85
Reagan, Ronald, 1, 113, 130
relocation of ethnic Japanese during World War II, ix, 111
rice cultivation, 74, 76n22; Wakamatsu and, 65, 69, 72–73, 74
Roosevelt, Franklin D., ix
Roosevelt, Theodore, 43, 46, 107
Russo-Japanese War, 26, 43, 107
Rutgers University, 42

Sacramento Daily Union, 53, 70–71
sakura, 117
Sakurai, Matsunosuke, 10, 92–93, 129; later life, 108–109
samurai: demographics of, 28n1; Sakurai as, 108; Schnell and, 32, 33; Shiba and, 26; and Wakamatsu Colony, 9–11, 58
samurai sword. *See* dagger found at Wakamatsu site
San Francisco Call, 73–74

Sasaki, Christen, 105
Satsuma Domain, 19, 20, 21–22, 25, 27, 28n16
Schnell, Edward: background of, 31–32; and California, 35; in Japan, 5, 32, 33; lack of information on, 13
Schnell family, later life, 6, 34, 78
Schnell, Frances, 5, 36n1, 52, 57
Schnell, John Henry, 2, 36n1; and Aizu Han, 31–34; background of, 31–32, 84; and decision to move to California, 34–35; on goal of colony, 65; in Japan, 5, 52; lack of information on, 31, 52; later life, 88, 128; and leadership, 35–36, 88; and press, 82
Schnell, Jou, 5, 6, 52, 57; background of, 33, 37n10, 58; press on, 47, 53
Schnell, Mary, 36n1, 51, 53, 57
Seiichi, Shima, 130
sericulture, 66; evaluation of, 80–81; Japan and, 67, 68; National Register on, 8; Wakamatsu Colony and, 69–72
Shiba, Gorō, 26–27
Shiraishi, Naori, 110
Shishi, 20
Sierra mountains, 84
silkworms, 6, 67, 69, 73
Sindryo family, 57
Sino-Japanese War, 26, 45
Sinsia family, 57
suicides: in Aizu Han, 25; Shiba and, 26

Taiping Rebellion, 39
Takahashi, Yoshio, 9, 10
Takaki, Ronald, 13
Taketa, Henry, 92, 102, 129
Tanimoto, Herb, 60, 109
Tasnezero, 57
tea cultivation, 6, 66, 75, 75n6; climate and, 70, 71; evaluation of, 80–81; Japan and, 67, 68–69; National Register on, 8; present day, 87; seeds, 52, 69, 71; Wakamatsu Colony and, 69–72, 74, 78–79
textile industry, Japanese, 68
Tobener, Anna Fredricka, 12
Toffelmier, Cynthia, 121–122
Toga, Yoich, 93
Tokugawa Ieyasu, 18

Tokugawa Shogunate, 18–19; collapse of, 19–21
Tokugawa Yoshinobu, 20, 28n16
Tomodgaro, 57
Torimoto, Ikuko, 12, 32
Totman, Conrad, 21
tozama daimyo, 20; definition of, 28n5
truck farming, 44, 65
Tsuginosuke, Kawa, 33
Tsugonusuke, Kawaii, 32
Tsuruga Castle, 24

Uchida, Yoshiko, 60
United States: and arms trade, 37n5; and Japan, 107; and tea market, 69; trade agreements with Japan, 19. *See also* American reactions to Japanese immigrants
Ushijima, Kinji, 44
utopian communities, 61–62, 126

Van Reed, Eugene, 41, 74
Van Sant, John E., 7, 12, 28n16; on dispersal of workers, 108; on Japanese immigration, 102; on land purchase, 62n12, 127; on Masumizu, 111; on Schnell in California, 35; on seriousness of colony, 40
Vassar College, 42
Veerkamp family, 10, 12, 109, 116, 124, 130; and Okei, 14, 92, 98, 102
Veerkamp, Francis, 124, 130
Veerkamp, Henry, 102
von Brandt, Max, 32, 37n2

Wakamatsu castle town, 24, 27
WakamatsuFest150, 118
Wakamatsu Japanese: 1870 census on, 56–57; departure of, 78, 83, 86; geographic origins of, 10; housing for, 59–60; labor contracts and wages, 35, 36, 59, 62, 86; lack of information on, 60–62; later life, 35, 36, 59, 87, 107–112, 129; numbers of, 10, 36, 37n17, 55–56, 71, 87; reception in U.S., 7–8, 39–40, 46–49; social origins of, 9–11, 34, 57, 58–59, 63n15
Wakamatsu Tea and Silk Colony Farm: as colony, 36; conservation of site, 113–119; founding of, 51–62; goal of, 2, 6, 65–75; historical background of, 5–7; importance of, 7–9, 124–125; land purchase for, 55–56, 62n12, 127–128, 133–134; memorial, 1; Miller on, x; outcome of, 77–88; as pilgrimage site, 101–105; planning, 11, 34, 51, 69–73, 82–83; property layout, 48, 56
water issues, 73; ARC and, 114–115; and fate of colony, 79–80, 83–85; importance of, 85
wax trees, 52, 69
Western imperialism: and Boshin War, 22–23; and Japan, 17–18
Wilde, Oscar, 61
Wilhelm II, kaiser of Germany, 45
Wilson, Carrie, 111, 129
wine industry, 66, 72
Wozezoro family, 57
Wright, Diana E., 25

Yamamoto, Yae, 24
Yanagisawa, Sakichi, 110–111
"yellow peril," 45, 46
Yoshida Shoin, 20

Zaibei Nihonjinshi, 94, 95

About the Author

Daniel A. Métraux is professor emeritus and adjunct professor of Asian studies at Mary Baldwin University in Staunton, Virginia. He holds a PhD from the Department of East Asian Studies at Columbia University. Dr. Métraux was a Fulbright scholar in Korea and Taiwan in 1988 and in China in 2006. He has taught as an exchange professor at Soka University in Tokyo and at Doshisha Women's College in Kyoto and was a visiting fellow at the Australian National University in 2002. Dr. Métraux has written many books, book chapters, and articles on Japanese and East Asian history, religion, and culture including *The Soka Gakkai Revolution* (1994), *Burma's Modern Tragedy* (2004), and *The Asian Writings of Jack London* (2010).

www.ingramcontent.com/pod-product-compliance
Lightning Source LLC
Chambersburg PA
CBHW050909300426
44111CB00010B/1447